BRAVE PAs

THE ULTIMATE GUIDE TO BEING OUTSTANDING IN A TOUGH JOB

To Sue,
The bravest of the brave!
with love from
Anne x

FOR PAs, EAs, SECRETARIES AND ADMINISTRATORS • WORKING IN EDUCATION

FROM THE WORLD'S MOST CONNECTED PERSONAL ASSISTANT AND PA TRAINER

ANGELA GARRY

 Independent Thinking Press

First published by

Independent Thinking Press
Crown Buildings, Bancyfelin, Carmarthen, Wales, SA33 5ND, UK
www.independentthinkingpress.com

Independent Thinking Press is an imprint of Crown House Publishing Ltd.

First published 2015.

British Library Cataloguing-in-Publication Data
A catalogue entry for this book is available
from the British Library.

Edited by Dave Harris.

Print ISBN 978-1-78135-221-2
Mobi ISBN 978-1-78135-222-9
ePub ISBN 978-1-78135-223-6
ePDF ISBN 978-1-78135-224-3

Printed and bound in the UK by
Gomer Press, Llandysul, Ceredigion

To my loved ones:

> You know who you are.
> You help me do what I do,
> and allow me to be who I am,
> whilst encouraging me to push myself
> to be the best that I can be.
> Thank you for being there for me when it really matters.

CONTENTS

FOREWORD

We live in a world where education has been swamped by deadlines, systems and procedures. Never has the school leader more needed assistance than now. Each day hundreds of emails, forms, submissions and phone calls bombard the leader's desk, and this is all before the children, staff, parents and governors each add in their own special demands. Without help most people would buckle, and sadly some do. This is where the importance of quality organisational support becomes clear: you need someone to help raise your head from the swamp, someone to take control. However, it would be a grave error to think that a quality PA is simply a way of removing paperwork and ticking boxes – a good one is so much more than this.

Many of us are worried that the human side of education is being hidden under a mass of numbers and targets, and that schools need to reclaim the moral purpose for education. I would argue this becomes much easier with a talented PA at your side.

In this book, Angela Garry skilfully identifies many of the essential skills that anyone wanting to step into this demanding role should be looking to develop. She adopts the metaphor of the PA's bag to guide us through the multifaceted demands of the role. Sometimes the ideas for the bag are small gems (like how to remember the tea and coffee order) whilst others could help save the school from disaster (like the advice on preparing for a major computer meltdown). After reading this book, every head teacher will be asking to see the 'purple folder' which Angela encourages her fellow PAs to prepare. She writes with an authoritative voice, born out of her wide and varied career, including her recent work training PAs across the globe. However, it would be wrong to imagine this as a simple factual 'how to' book; Angela writes with real heart, and she uses humour and honesty to get her message over.

Angela loved her time working in schools and that is clear from her writing, but she also doesn't shy away from addressing some of the problems that anyone working in a school office role might meet. She expresses the humanity that the role requires and describes with real colour some of the situations that will occur, but importantly, for each, she gives practical ideas about what you can do about them.

Schools need a brave and talented office team supporting the work of the school. In fact, I doubt any school can be successful without one. The role of a head teacher can be very demanding and lonely (I know – I've been there!), but the role becomes less stressful with a brave PA by your side. Someone prepared to work efficiently under the radar, someone who can go places you can't, someone who hears things you can't, someone who helps you keep your many plates spinning.

Education is definitely not about the numbers – it's about the people. *Brave PAs* should be read, not only by every PA, EA, secretary and administrator working in education, but by every leader who wants to create a school, college or university which is focused on this.

Dave Harris
former head teacher and author of *Are You Dropping the Baton?*,
Brave Heads and co-author of *Leadership Dialogues*

INTRODUCTION

It takes a lot to be a great administrator in an educational environment – nay, it takes real bravery. It's not the same as working in a personal assistant (PA), executive assistant (EA), secretarial or administrative role in any other environment. We work to distinctly different customer groups, and ultimately the aim of our institution is not all about profit – it's about developing our pupils and students into the citizens of tomorrow. We are part of an institution that is helping to develop the next generation's rocket scientists, cleaners, doctors, bus drivers, shop workers, industrialists, firemen, inventors and parents of generations to follow – plus all those whom we will inspire to become budding PAs!

Imagine, if you will, that we all have within us a small velvet bag that is filled with a handful of little glass beads. Each bead contains the essence of one of our brave strengths, assets and skills – our internal 'Bravery SAS'. This is where our bravery comes from, based on how we use these beads: one at a time or in combination with other beads.

Some people carry their bravery bag deep inside their pocket, hidden away, and don't bring it out into the open very often, believing that there is a limit on usage and they must reserve it only for special occasions. Some people aren't even aware that they have a bravery bag, so never use it. Some open their bravery bag and look through the beads, choosing to select just a few of them. Others wear their bravery bag on their shoulder and rummage through it on a regular basis.

Brave PAs use their bravery bag daily and will find that they use every bead within the bag at some point, sometimes using several at once to find brave solutions and methods to meet their various challenges. Each of the 48 chapters in this book looks at one or more of the different bravery skills, assets and strengths required to be successful in your role: what they are and how you can use them, how you can supplement and develop them, and how to make sure you access them on a regular basis to become a brave PA in education.

This book is based on my experiences of training to be a teacher and subsequently working in administrative, secretarial and PA roles in education. *Brave PAs* offers a selection of my tips, hints, anecdotes, time-savings, advice, knowledge and expertise to assist with your continuing professional development, and to enable you to be the best you can be in your role, bravely supporting the leadership of your school, college or university.

You might choose to read just one chapter of this book per week, and think of this book as a guide for use throughout an academic year in your role, or you might prefer to dip in and out of it at random. Alternatively, you may like to pick out chapters on a particular topic (see the topic list at the back of the book). Whatever you do with it, I hope that it helps you in your role as a PA in education. There are so many more chapters I could have included (I started out with a list of more than 70!) on so many more aspects of working in an educational environment – but this seemed enough for starters.

Note: *Brave PAs* has been written specifically for PAs, EAs, secretaries and administrative staff working in schools, colleges and universities. Throughout the book, the terms 'PA', 'head teacher' and 'school' are used as shortcuts for all administrative staff and their head teachers/principals/college leaders/university heads/leaders in other educational institutions.

All anecdotal evidence within this book is true – but names have been changed to preserve anonymity where requested.

BRAVERY IS ...

BRAVERY IS ... STEPPING INTO YOUR FIRST ROLE IN AN EDUCATIONAL ENVIRONMENT

Your first experiences of working in an educational environment may well be scary, whether you are arriving straight from school or college or from working in a role in a different industry. Many people believe that a job in education will be 'easier' than elsewhere, that they will enjoy long holidays and short hours, but this generally does not prove to be the case!

With increasingly smaller budgets and tighter controls on spending, educational institutions are becoming pressurised into becoming 'lean', which means reducing staff numbers and overheads whilst still maintaining standards and delivering excellent teaching for the students. The role of PA, EA or secretary in a school, college or university is often therefore a hugely responsible position, which will require you to have lots of fingers in lots of different pies throughout the organisation, regardless of whether your job is to support just one individual or many staff members. You will become involved in the whole organisation for the good of all – and so you should! The better acquainted you can become with the workings and machinations of your school or college, the better you will be able to support its leadership.

PAs who make the move from a corporate role will be used to working in busy, pressurised situations, but many will be unprepared for the sheer number of interruptions that will occur during the working day in education, as pupils, parents, teachers, teaching assistants, governors, professors, college sponsors, community members and many more compete for their attention. I've spent my career working in corporate, charity and educational institutions, and I've seen the huge gulf between what people think of as a 'cushy number' working in education in comparison with what actually happens.

Please don't get me wrong. I'm not saying that working in education is an awful experience, too hard, too difficult or too pressurised. I have loved each and every one of my roles as an administrator in education – as, I am sure, will you – and I have felt challenged to push myself to reach high standards throughout. It's always been a role where I have felt valued and where I have known that what I was doing was working towards an overall goal that is sincerely worthwhile – educating the adults of the next generation. I love the PA role and working in the educational sphere with equal passion. And, with each job, I have developed different skills and new methods of working.

Education is a very different experience than working anywhere else. There are very few other organisations where you would be required to deal with huge numbers of children, teenagers and young adults every day in your workplace, as well as 'already grown' adults. For those who have spent their career working solely with adults, it can be a daunting or scary experience to make the switch to working in education. It takes bravery.

My experiences of working in educational environments have required bravery throughout, to adapt to the various demands required of me as a PA, an adult, a tutor, a coach, a mentor, a member of the local community; bravery which I'm going to share with you over the coming pages, and which I hope can help you in your future as a brave PA in education.

BRAVERY IS ... ENLIGHTENING
– SOME LIGHT-HEARTED ADVICE FOR A NEW PA

If you are brand new to being a PA, then welcome to this really exciting profession!

Being a new PA or administrative assistant is no easy task. Your head teacher or principal will quite often expect things of you that you are unfamiliar with – they may presume that you already know what to do without being told. They will probably also expect that you automatically know their preferences and will be able to organise logistics successfully on their behalf.

If you want to be great at your job, the following enlightenments should be useful to you.

BE FRIENDLY AND EARN THE RESPECT OF YOUR COLLEAGUES

When you arrive in a new role, your colleagues need to know who you are and what you do. If you need something from them, you need them to respond accordingly. A major element of the PA role is chasing people to get them to produce reports and papers to deadline, to agree to attend meetings, to turn up on time and to take on extra responsibility, so you need your colleagues to know that you are there as the head's or principal's 'third arm'. You are there to ensure that whatever needs doing gets done.

You will need to get to know about the people your boss will meet with on a regular basis – this might by the school or college's governors, or the university's council. If they are familiar with who you are and what your role is, a good working relationship with them should develop much easier than if they have no idea who you are or what you are doing. You may not be directly involved with their schedule or time management, but getting acquainted with their assistants will help assure their cooperation when you need something from them.

MOST LIKELY, YOUR COLLEAGUES KNOW NOTHING ABOUT WHAT A PA DOES

You will find that many of the people you work with have little idea about the role of a PA so your task should be to educate them! They may think of you as a diary-keeper, a chaser-of-deadlines or the 'go to' person for everything under the sun, so they will often come to you with questions or tasks that aren't your responsibility to fulfil, but they have no idea who else to go to with them, so they come to you. Of course, these are things that you will take in your stride in time – it is usually a case of 'If you don't know who to ask about something, ask the PA – they will be able to find out for you'. For example, many of your colleagues will be under the impression that you are (apparently) the only person in the entire world who knows where anything is. Without you, nobody would know who to call, when the meeting is or who it is with – and the list keeps going.

Being a PA (and a brave one at that!) requires certain skills including organising meetings, handling travel itineraries, having good (or preferably great) computing skills and typing speeds, as well as being flexible and adaptable to working with last minute changes. But, because of their lack of knowledge about the role, a lot of people assume that the role of PA is easy, which is rather hilarious. I have never met (nor heard of) a PA who has described their job as easy.

Your role at this point is to enlighten your colleagues. Become an ambassador for the profession and demonstrate to them the true power of the PA – that we essentially control the head teacher's time. We decide if and when someone may see our boss or speak to them by phone. We keep the head teacher or principal supported in a safety net that allows them to walk the tightrope of running the organisation, secure in the knowledge that we've 'got their back'.

Here are some of the key skills that you will need to succeed as a brave PA.

YOU NEED TO BE AN ELEPHANT

You know the saying, 'Elephants never forget'? PAs must not forget anything because there is nobody to back you up. People will come to you looking for a piece of paper they had in their hand six weeks ago or for the contact details of someone who visited the school last term, and even if you had nothing to do with the original details you will be expected to find out.

Your head teacher or principal will ask you to 'dig out' an email they received from John or Bob, (or was it Phil?), three or four weeks ago, which mentioned something about X or Y. Undoubtedly, it will turn out to have been a message from Simon, which mentioned that Tim might be involved in a project (to which the head had thought, 'No, that's Bob's responsibility'), but you will have to work this out by remembering the conversation you had with the head that day when he mentioned something about Bob …

To become great PAs, we need to develop an almost ESP-type connection with our bosses to work out what it is they mean, because quite often they do not tell us or give us the wrong information. Great detective skills also help to piece together the fragments of information that we gather every day.

YOU NEED TO KNOW EVERYTHING ABOUT EVERYONE

It will also be expected that you know everyone's needs, wants, quirks, habits, demands and eccentricities, because you will, of course, have developed an encyclopaedic knowledge of the staff within the first few moments of having arrived in your new role!

YOU NEED TO BE THE BEST TRAVEL ORGANISER

As well as organising meetings you will quite often be the travel arranger. Anyone who has booked a business trip for six people, all flying from different airports at different times, and all having different personal preferences about the type of place where they want to stay, will be able to tell you that booking travel can be unbelievably complicated – and you will be expected to be the person who can magically make it all happen.

YOU NEED TO BE A GREAT EVENT ORGANISER

As a PA, you will be the person to organise the next conference or major meeting. Whilst it's highly possible that you enjoy event planning and organising (I do hope so!), nobody around you will have any idea how hard it actually is to organise a full conference. All those who do have an inkling will usually steer clear and leave it to you, as you are the 'trained professional'. This being the case, try to get your name down for a course on event management to help you along.

YOU NEED TO MANAGE TIME CAREFULLY AND WISELY

There are many different aspects to the role of PA, but one of the most important is that of managing time. And by that I mean both yours *and* the person you work for.

You will need to be quick and accurate in the work that you do, adaptable to be able to pick up different tasks at different times and fastidious enough to make sure that nothing gets left behind. You will undoubtedly have a task list a mile long, and it can be quite daunting to a new PA to be suddenly expected to manage this.

In addition, you need to make sure that your head teacher has time to meet with people, speak with them on the phone and do all of the necessary things that are involved in running a busy school or college. This means that you will need your calendar synced with theirs, as you will be responsible for ensuring that they get to those meetings at the right time, with the right papers, with the right travel arrangements and know who they are meeting and why. Your IT team will be able to set it up so that your calendars can work together.

As well as ensuring that your head gets to the right meetings, you will be involved in making sure that those meetings happen without a hitch, requiring attention to details such as everyone's availability, preparing papers for the meeting and making sure that everything from the conception of the meeting up to the moment it ends goes smoothly.

Once you've got a handle on their calendar, you will probably also need some sort of access to your head teacher's emails too, but very early on in a PA role, particularly for a new PA, this may not be a requirement just yet.

ONE OF THE MAJOR CHALLENGES OF THE ROLE IS TO SHINE

In the words of REM, PAs are always 'shiny happy people'. Or at least, we're not supposed to answer the phone or greet visitors at the door with, 'What do you want?' Always aim to shine and be happy to meet the people who come into your room, who call you on the phone, who pass you in the corridor or outside visitors who come into your school, college or university. We are there to welcome people into the organisation, and to give them a positive impression of what we collectively do for the pupils and students.

Remember that a key element in being a great PA is enjoying your work. It's not a role that everyone is suited to, because of the enormous amount of multi-tasking required, but it can be incredibly rewarding. No matter what happens, we will either fix it, sort it out or will know how or who to get it done.

Welcome to the role of PA – buckle up, strap yourself in, it's going to be an exciting ride! And don't forget to use your role to enlighten others.

BRAVERY IS ... GETTING
OFF TO A GREAT FIRST START

Some of the first things you will need to do in the first few days in your new role include:

FINDING, READING AND DIGESTING THE HANDOVER NOTES FROM YOUR PREDECESSOR

What do you mean, there aren't any handover notes? Check the shelves and drawers in your new office – is there a purple coloured folder anywhere? (A note for your future self: whenever you leave a job, leave behind some excellent handover notes for your successor – see page 215.)

All too often we start at a new job and have to think on our feet on the first day because the person who left the job didn't leave any notes behind. If you find that this is the case when you start a job, make sure that you *do not* do this to your successor when you leave!

OK, so you've read the handover notes (or not, as the case may be). What's next?

GETTING SET UP AND FINDING OUT THE BASICS

- Get set up for computer access. You will need a username and password, access to the network and someone to tell you what's where within the system.

- Telephone access. Do you need a pin number to sign in to the voicemail system? How do you set up speed dials on your desk phone? What is already set up on it? With luck, this should be detailed in the handover notes you receive.

- Access to the boss's email/calendar via the computer network. Some managers will want you to have 'viewing' access only while you and they build up trust; others will expect and need you to have full 'editing' access straightaway.

- Where is the toilet/staffroom/break area?

- What is the routine for lunches – how do you pay? How often? What time? Where do you go?

- Is there a safe place for your personal belongings during the day (e.g. a locker or a lockable drawer in your desk)?

- Fire/emergency evacuation procedures – where should you go, and what should you do?

- Where are the tea and coffee supplies/printing supplies/ stationery cupboard?

- Where are the keys to the filing cabinets in your workspace or office?

- Do you need keys to the office and/or security cards to 'swipe' your way into the building?

GETTING COMFORTABLE

Set about rearranging your room and setting up your desk how you want it, including hunting out a more comfortable chair, if necessary, as you are likely to be sitting at your desk for some very long hours at times! Move things around until you are comfortable with them.

For example, I'm used to working with two screens, with a laptop in front of me and a second monitor and my desk phone to the right, plus a full-size keyboard and mouse in front of the laptop. Trying to work at a desk where the computer and phone are on the wrong side of the desk means I can't work at my best capacity, as I get neck strain from leaning to the left. I have worked with a number of people who have spent years working in uncomfortable positions like this, without resolving the issue by simply moving things around.

Where is the main source of natural light/electronic light in the room? Do you need to move the actual location of your desk in the room so that you are not blinded by sunlight for certain parts of the day? I've worked with PAs who sit squinting all afternoon in the autumn – when the sun starts to set at just the wrong angle for them to be comfortable – and quite often they haven't moved their desk to alleviate this, saying it would be too troublesome to do. However, squinting in the wrong lighting and getting headaches isn't worth it – so get the desk moved!

INSTALLING USEFUL STUFF

You may have used various computing aids or shortcuts in previous jobs, such as autocorrects, short words and dictionaries. Now is the time to put them in place in your new role. Also add commonly used work-related website addresses to your browser's favourites list. If you have done your homework in your last job, you will have created copies of these to bring with you before you left. (For more on this, see pages 117 and 215.)

Check what computing packages are available to you on your new computer – for example, you may be a whizz with Microsoft Project and used it on a regular basis in your old job, but may find that it's not installed on your computer in your new job. If you anticipate that you are going to need it (and let's face it, you probably will) then you will need to get on to your IT team to see if it can be installed. If the software is already available within the school then this should not be a problem, but if it has to be purchased you may need to justify the purchase to your head or finance team, as well as the IT team.

COMPILING YOUR NEW JOB'S VITAL STATISTICS

If the following information has not been provided, then find out your boss's car make/model/registration number, their mobile number, home phone number, their partner's mobile number, name/phone number of their children's schools, contact numbers for their doctor/dentist/parents, the garage for their car and so on. You will also need the desk phone numbers and mobile numbers of the leadership team and the board of directors or governing body (if your role includes working with these). Obtain a list from your colleagues, or start compiling one yourself.

WHO'S WHO?

One massively important thing for you to do early on in your new role is to work out who everyone is. Get hold of whatever organisation structure diagram you can find. Ask your boss – or the human resources department – for this. If your predecessor has done their job well, they will have included a copy in their handover notes. If there isn't one, start compiling one and get it printed out and up on your wall as soon as you possibly can. It doesn't have to be fancy – just use the basic organisation chart tool within Word if you have to, or draw it up on a piece of paper – but having something that identifies who works where, and for whom, is vital.

Check it through with your boss and ask if you have the reporting lines marked up correctly. More than likely they will be pleased that you are using your initiative in creating something that is badly needed within the organisation. Once you have an organisation chart in front of you, start working your way around it – getting to know who everyone is and checking out their roles and responsibilities: who works with whom, in which teams, and who reports to whom.

If you have a staff photo list, print it out and stick it on your wall, and use it alongside the structure diagram. If you don't have a staff photo list, check with whoever creates your staff security badges and ask for access to the photos of staff. This will be a godsend to you in the first few weeks in a new role, as you can look up the person you just chatted with at lunchtime and work out their relationship to your role.

KEEP A LIST OF IMPORTANT PEOPLE, AND BE SURE TO KEEP IT UP-TO-DATE

You will find that building a database of dignitaries and invited guests for the annual gala awards ceremony for pupils will take time but, most importantly, you need to remember that whatever list you create should be reviewed and amended year in, year out.

The people outside of the school who were deemed 'important' five years ago may not be the most appropriate individuals to invite to an event taking place now, when the school, the staffing, the curriculum (and often that person's involvement and interest in the school) have all moved on in different directions.

All of the above details, once you've compiled them, should feed into your purple folder, as you develop it.

MAKING SOME VERY IMPORTANT NEW 'BUDDIES'

Whenever you start a new job, one of the first things you need to do is to meet, greet and get to know your team of best buddies – the people who will help you out at the crucial times throughout the coming years. Generally, this team consists of:

- The IT expert – who can reboot the server or kick-start a faulty laptop at a moment's notice.

- The reprographics expert – in charge of the copying facilities.

- The site officer/caretaker – the holder of the keys to the building and the access codes for the security system, and the person who can put up signage for events and reserve parking spaces for any important guests.

- The chef/catering manager – the key to everyone's stomachs, including refreshments for meetings.

- The receptionist(s) – who will usually be the font of all knowledge about the whole organisation.

Seek out these people, find out their names, memorise them and make friendly working relationships with them. There will be times when you desperately need their assistance – when the computer network breaks down just a few minutes before a vital meeting, when a huge amount of copying simply *has* to be done at late notice, when the building needs to be kept open until late one evening in order to help you get a tender or bid completed on time, when a large party of visitors descend on the organisation and are in need of urgent refreshments, or when you are waiting for a special VIP visitor but you don't want to be seen hanging around waiting for them in the foyer of the building.

Like I've said, make friends with these people. Add them to your personal Christmas card list, give them a bottle of wine or a box of chocolates on their birthday, bring them back a little 'silly something' from your holiday abroad – and get on their good side. Thank them for their assistance and always let them know how much you appreciate their help. This is most definitely not a case of sucking up to people – this is a case of rapidly building good working relationships with the individuals who will be vital to you throughout your role in this school/college.

Always thank your buddies for their assistance and let them know how much you appreciate their help. Always give credit where it is due and make sure your colleagues get recognition from others for their efforts – for example, ask the boss to say a special thank you to them during a staff meeting or find a way to praise them in the school or college newsletter.

Ultimately, everyone in the organisation will be important to you in some way, but these five people will tend to be amongst the most important – they are your new 'A Team', your best buddies.

WORKING WITH EVERYONE ELSE

Build your relationships with everyone in the school slowly and at a steady pace. Everything we do has a knock-on effect further down the line ... The little Year 7 boy who has banged constantly on your door every breaktime this week, and is becoming a bit of a pest, will in all too short a time become one of the school's GCSE pupils in Year 10 or 11. If, during his Year 7, you scared him away from your office and told him not to bother you, he may not feel willing, three or four years down the line, to come to you with his concerns about a fellow pupil who needs some help.

Taking time to listen to a parent when she phones in, worried about her child's report, will make all the difference to that parent when you later send out a request for people to volunteer to work with pupils in an after-hours group. Because you have been a caring and supportive ear, she may feel more inclined to offer her assistance.

The same applies to connections outside the school. For example, building up a good working relationship during the year with a stationery supplier will undoubtedly pay dividends when you are asked to source something at extremely short notice – because you have nurtured that relationship, you should be able to persuade them to send an urgent item to you via courier to meet that vital deadline, and still negotiate a lower price with them.

All of these things can make a difference to someone, somewhere. Let it be you that makes it happen.

TAKING IT GENTLY

A word of caution on starting in your new job in a school, college, university – or, indeed, anywhere. I've met a few PAs in the past who have started at a new job by blasting their way in, as if through concrete. They have barged in on conversations, shoved their point forward in discussions and pushed themselves to the forefront in an effort to try to gain the immediate recognition and respect of their colleagues.

One PA who joined a university where I was working told me on her first day that she wanted to make it clear that she was 'a force to be reckoned with', and that when she asked for something to be done (on behalf of the team of professors for whom she worked) she wanted everyone on the staff to know that it 'jolly well ought to be done, sharp-ish'. My hackles went straight up at this, and I would strongly recommend against this sort of approach.

Admittedly, being a PA is not the best role in which to make yourself lots of lovely, fluffy, cuddly friends within the workforce. You should aim to be friendly with your colleagues, and any actual friendships that form can be considered a bonus (and a hindrance at times!), but you would definitely do well not to go out of your way during your first few days to make any enemies.

If you are starting a new job in education, in the early days, you are likely to meet other people in other roles who know much more about the organisation than you do, and who will not appreciate being bullied or harassed. Make a slower, stronger, sleeker approach to building working relationships with your fellow staff. After all, if things go well you could be in this role and working alongside these people for many years to come, so work on making a really positive start.

BRAVERY IS ... REALISING YOU ARE NOT 'JUST A PA' – YOUR DESK IS THE CENTRAL COG AROUND WHICH THE REST OF THE SCHOOL'S MACHINERY REVOLVES

In your role as PA to the leader of a school, college or university, you will make a difference to the work and lives of those around you, pretty much by simply being there. You will ease the lives of others by arranging much needed meetings with your boss, handling queries from those who have no idea where else to go with their questions, sorting out problems that don't 'fit' within other departments and dealing with students, parents and other concerned parties in a professional and methodical manner.

For my part, I always knew that my roles in education were really important – providing the vital link between principals, professors, deputy vice chancellors and everyone else at a huge range of levels in an institution: leadership teams, professors, committees, tutors, students, their families, governing bodies, sponsors and so on. I'm really proud that what I did on a day-to-day basis was helping to provide a form of education that was truly innovative and out of the ordinary. I got great satisfaction from knowing that I was making a difference.

My hope is that you can gain that feeling of satisfaction in your role too – enjoying what you do, feeling appreciated and knowing that you too make a difference.

After the head/principal, their assistants are quite possibly the most important staff members when it comes to running the school or college. Some people might counter this by pointing out that a school or college PA doesn't deliver the curriculum – they don't stand up in the classrooms and teach – and the key business of the institute is to teach. My response is that we are the glue that holds everything together, the central cog in the machinery, the conduit through which the electricity flows. As the head/principal is linked with all the departments of the institution, so are we, which puts us in a unique position amongst the staff, because we know the confidential 'ins and outs' of the whole institution!

We are also in a key position to influence the decision-makers on a huge range of issues. We are the head teacher's 'third arm', and our role is to support them in whatever they do. This means we need to know a great deal about what they know, what they do and how they do it in order to work well with them and provide the support that they need. As a PA, EA or secretary you are effectively an extension of the head teacher, their second voice within the school or college.

To be a great PA in a school or college you need to create good working relationships with the staff in every department. They need to know that you are supporting them in their jobs through the support you give to the head teacher. They also need to know that you are acting on behalf of the head teacher, and that if you are asking them to do something, this usually means that you are asking them on behalf of the head.

By creating and maintaining good relationships with the staff, and by demonstrating your enthusiasm for, and commitment to, for your role, you can also be a good motivator to others.

BRAVERY IS ... TAKING
ON TASKS THAT WOULDN'T BE EXPECTED IN A CORPORATE PA JOB

If you have worked as a PA in the commercial world this will in no way hold you back if you are looking to move into an educational environment. But please don't expect your day to be anywhere near as easy to divide up into a manageable structure!

> I've spent half my career in education and the other half in corporate, industrial and charity roles. I have also spoken with a large number of PAs who have had prior experience of working in PA roles outside of education. The general consensus is that day-to-day life in an educational institution is very different from working elsewhere. Yes, there are similarities in the types of tasks and roles that we undertake as PAs or administrators in any working environment, but the educational setting requires so much more of us, and the level of responsibility for people can be far greater.

The most basic example of the difference is the number of interruptions that you will undoubtedly experience in your school or college office, such as phone calls from parents, drop-in visits from parents or pupils and tutors popping in. This will occur much more frequently than anything you are likely to have experienced elsewhere.

In a corporate environment, what we do in our jobs as PAs has a direct impact on the daily routine of the individual executive(s) for whom we work. We may have links with the board of directors and the rest of the staff, but that is usually where the 'spread' of our role stops.

In a school, college or university, this same set-up is mirrored in that we report to the head teacher, principal or director, plus we may be required to work with the board of governors or the various committees and councils running the college or university. We will also work with the other staff in the institution. However, we also have an impact on the education of every single one of the school pupils, college students or undergraduates with whom we come into contact, and in the school setting we also come into regular contact with their parents, siblings and other family members.

If you're working in a corporate environment, I don't suppose you will have ever experienced having to supervise a group of children or cope with a crying parent as a sudden, unexpected but wholly necessary part of your daily tasks, but it is commonplace in education!

COPING WITH THE UNFAMILIAR

So, what might you experience, and how might you handle it? Let's take a typical Tuesday after lunch when a pupil walks into your office:

You: Hello, can I help you?

Pupil: Miss, I've been sent to see the principal.

You: He's in a meeting right now.

Pupil: Can I go then? I wasn't doing anything. It's not my fault …

This is likely to happen to you many times. The first few occasions may feel unnerving, especially if you have not already thought about what you will do in this instance. You probably won't be used to having children sitting in your office with you, so what do you do?

Firstly, make a space for them to sit down and give them something to do so that they are occupied and you can carry on with your work while you wait for the principal to become free. Perhaps move some things off a low cupboard or a small table and pull up a chair. Then give them some paper and a pen, and say something like, 'I tell you what, sit here with me and let's start on getting this sorted out while you wait for the principal.'

By this point, the pupil may well start to tell you what's happened. Ideally, it is best for you to remain impartial, so set them a task, which will allow you to return to your own work, by saying something like, 'I can't really get involved in what's gone on, that's between you and your teacher, but a good thing for you to do now would be to write a statement of what happened while it's all fresh in your mind.'

To make sure they know what you mean, ask them: 'You know what a statement is, right? I bet you've seen it on police shows on TV. You write down everything that happened. How it started, what was said by whom, who did what and what led to you being sent to the principal's office. You do that, and it will give your side of what happened. Make sure you include everything that you think is relevant. That way, when he is free, you can tell the principal everything clearly because you will have had time to go through it on paper, and put your best case forward about what happened and why.'

In most cases, the pupil will sit and write whilst you carry on with a task at your desk, although sometimes they will just sit there staring sullenly at the piece of paper. Tell them that you are not taking sides with anyone, and you aren't going to argue with them or be drawn into discussing the incident, and they will probably get on with it.

With the few pupils who absolutely refuse to write a statement, put a book in front of them and ask them to write out a couple of pages from it or, as a very last resort, to read it. For this purpose, I'd suggest you ask the maths and English departments to give you a couple of textbooks to keep in the cupboard or maybe consider bringing something in from your own collection.

Another example of a task you wouldn't expect to carry out in a non-education role is dealing with angry calls from parents who might be upset that their application for a space for their child has been rejected. (See page 171 for more on answering angry or upset calls from parents.) A couple of days after your local authority's admissions office has sent out letters to all Year 6 parents on their success (or failure in the case of over-subscribed schools) to gain a place for their child in September's Year 7 entry to the school, your phone might ring:

 In my office I had a small shelf containing a range of books, from maths activities (from my degree course in teaching) and Greek and Roman myths to the *Guinness Book of British Hit Singles* and a couple of novels. The school had very low rates of literacy, and my reasoning was that if I couldn't get a pupil to do any schoolwork, then the least I could do was to try to encourage them to read something whilst they were in my office as this might aid in some way to raise their literacy skills.

> You: Good morning, this is the principal's office. How can I help?
>
> Angry parent: Why hasn't my daughter got a place? She's been crying all night and I can't explain it to her. I want to talk to the principal.

In many schools, the head's/principal's PA is responsible for handling some aspects of admissions applications. If your school is over-subscribed, this sort of call will undoubtedly become familiar to you. In each case, you will need to carefully explain the various processes that were involved, share with them some information about the number of applications that were received and make it clear that, unfortunately, your school does not have spaces for everyone who applied.

In some cases, the parents may choose to submit a formal appeal, and you could well find yourself attending an official appeals meeting alongside the principal, or providing the principal with a whole ream of paperwork to support the school's case, which needs to be presented to an impartial panel of adjudicators and the parents.

As a PA in education, you may also find yourself talking with groups of parents at open evenings and school performances, briefing undergraduates from your local university who are coming in to volunteer part-time in the school, completing Disclosure and Barring Service (DBS) applications for parents who wish to attend as adult guides on a school trip or showing a local MP or councillor, plus their guests, around your school building during the summer holidays when the principal is away, thereby acting as an ambassador for the school in their absence.

You may also be involved in a whole range of other aspects of the students' learning: from my own experience of college and university roles, this could include undertaking tasks such as assisting undergraduates and postgraduates with research projects, driving around university halls of residence delivering leaflets about a forthcoming conference led by one of the professors I worked for, or being roped in to create the advertising materials (leaflets, posters, tickets, photography, etc.) for the drama department's student plays.

Other aspects of your role could include:

- Working on committees, including academic boards, governing bodies and task groups.
- Assisting with recruitment, public or alumni relations and marketing activities.
- Administering the 'student life cycle' from registration or admission to graduation or leaving.
- Providing administrative support to an academic team of lecturers, tutors or teachers.
- Drafting and interpreting regulations and dealing with queries and complaints procedures.
- Coordinating examination and assessment processes.

- Maintaining high levels of quality assurance, including course evaluation and course approval procedures.

- Using information systems and preparing reports and statistics for internal and external use.

- Participating in the development of future information systems.

- Contributing to policy and planning.

- Managing budgets and ensuring financial systems are followed.

- Purchasing goods and equipment, as required, and processing invoices.

- Supervising staff.

- Liaising with other administrative staff, academic colleagues and students.

- Liaising with partner institutions, other institutions, external agencies, government departments and prospective students.

- Organising and facilitating a variety of educational or social activities.

I can almost guarantee that you simply wouldn't get this level of variety, responsibility and involvement in a corporate PA role!

BRAVERY IS ... LEARNING SOMETHING NEW EVERY DAY/WEEK/MONTH

Throughout your role as a PA or administrator, you will always be learning something new or a different way to do something. It might be practical things like finding out how to change the toner in the photocopier, establishing a new method for receiving visitors at the school (think: visitor book, loose paper register, computerised database, finger-touch screen, iPad app, biometric finger-scanning system for repeat visitors, scanning DBS papers), developing your own systems for filing and retrieving documents or searching the internet for answers – or at least clues – on how to solve an issue.

Your learning might also be adding to or developing some of the vital 'soft skills' required to fulfil your role, such as interpersonal skills, building relationships, learning to adapt your working styles to fit best with your head teacher, developing ways to handle upset or angry parents and so on. It's always hard to start a job somewhere new and be expected to hit the ground running. However, being able to connect with others in similar roles elsewhere, borrow from their skills and learn from their experience can be invaluable.

We would be foolish to think that any of us knows everything there is to know about doing our jobs brilliantly. There has to be something more that you could learn within your role that would help you to support your head teacher or principal even better than you already do – something that might speed up a process, a new computing tool that will put you on a par with the pupils who are already using it or simply working on a new task that you have been given.

I'm absolutely certain that we *all* need to be constantly learning new things, not just for our own professional development but to keep up with the next generation who are part of our school, college or university.

 Over the years, I have met a very small number of PAs, secretaries and administrators who seemed to think they were so perfect in their roles that they did not need to learn anything more ('I am already great') or anything new ('My knowledge and skills may be old but they are great'). I have to admit that I find this quite a limiting approach to working (not to mention life itself!), and I've thought their views of their roles and responsibilities were more than a bit old-fashioned.

For instance, at a training course where I was introducing the assembled audience of PAs to the use of Gantt charts, one PA related that she had just helped her 10-year-old son with his homework the night before – and the homework was to create a Gantt chart. There was I, training a group of PAs in their thirties (and above) to use technology that 10-year-olds are currently being taught to use in school!

In another example, I recently came across a photo on Facebook of my cousin's baby boy, sitting on his grandpa's lap with a look of utter fascination on his face, whilst his grandpa showed him something on an iPhone. I recognised something in the look on the baby's face and dug through my old photo albums, where I found a photo of myself in the early 1970s, at the same age, with the same look of fascination on my face. I was not focused on an iPhone or any sort of new technology though – I was playing with a small red balloon. How times change! My cousin's son is growing up in a world where it is the norm to own a device which not only enables us to communicate with the rest of the world by phone call, text or the internet, but also play games and take photographs and videos. We have to continue learning to keep up with new advances in technology, otherwise we will be completely left behind.

WHAT SKILLS MIGHT YOU NEED TO DEVELOP IN ORDER TO BE A GREAT BRAVE PA?

- Multi-tasking
- Communication skills
- Negotiating
- Influencing
- Diary management
- Organisational skills
- Diplomacy and discretion
- Self-motivation
- Demonstrating initiative
- Attention to detail
- Networking
- Problem-solving

Some of these are touched on elsewhere in this book – others you will develop all by yourself, simply by spending time in your role, learning from and watching others.

WHAT IS YOUR PREFERRED LEARNING METHOD?

When you are going to attempt to learn something new, an important thing to take account of is to think about how you learn best, because each of us acquires skills and knowledge slightly differently. You may have been at school with friends who seemed to pick up things far more easily than you did, or perhaps you were the one who went racing ahead through the textbooks while your friends struggled. If you are going to undertake any new training or studying, it makes sense to ensure that it's delivered via a method that works well for you, so that it has the greatest impact.

It is often said that there are just two main learning methods: *active* and *passive*.

Active learning is about doing, initiative, exploring and testing. Examples include:

- Doing – coaching, project work, individual workshops, simulation
- Initiative – e-learning, workshops, open learning, quality competitions
- Exploring – mentoring, open learning, project work, quality competitions
- Testing – workshops

Passive learning is about observing, questioning, and reviewing. Examples include:

- Observing – job shadowing
- Questioning – induction, networking, seminars, evening classes
- Reviewing – individual workshops

Once you have identified your preferred learning style, try to look for courses that will be delivered in this style, so that you can get the most from the programme. Don't necessarily rule out courses delivered in the other styles if these are the only ones available to you, but if you get the option of attending more than one course, aim for whatever seems to match your learning style closest.

ACCELERATING YOUR LEARNING

Since each of us learns differently, we each need to develop techniques that exactly match our preferred learning style. This means we will learn faster, quicker and better – that is, the learning process is accelerated. Since this learning process doesn't happen overnight (it does take effort!), there are a few things you can do to speed up the process:

- Motivate yourself. See yourself learning in your mind, tell yourself that you will be successful in your learning and set goals for which you can strive.

- Get the information. There are three ways in which people learn from and interact with the world around them: visual (seeing), auditory (hearing), and kinaesthetic (touching/feeling). When you use the best way for you, you will be able to get the information you need faster in order to learn the task at hand.

- Find meaning. When you can relate to what you are learning, you will absorb the information faster and retain the knowledge longer.

- Use your memory. Task yourself with trying to recall everything you can. If necessary, get some help with memory techniques. The more you draw on the information, the easier it becomes to apply when it is needed.

- Actively do it. Try applying what you have learned as soon as you can and as often as possible. Repeating something over and over reinforces it in your mind and body, and it is said that if you repeat something daily for 28 days you can even turn it into a habit!

- Think about it. As you learn, you will make mistakes – we all will. It's important to go back and review what went well, and what went not so well, so that the next learning experience will be all the more successful.

Here are two routes to some fantastic resources to help you develop your learning:

- **www.bookboon.com** – an invaluable source of 'how to' books. Create a free registration to use on the site and then download e-books (saved in PDF format) on an enormous number of topics, including business/office subjects (e.g. comprehensive books on using the Microsoft Office suite – every package, every version – from beginner to intermediate to advanced level). The site has over 1,000 books available – some free, some on a fee-paying basis.

- **www.alison.com** – a training website offering online diploma courses. Create a free registration to use the site and sign up for a course. Free use of the site includes advertisements during your course sessions, or you can choose to pay for a premium subscription which will exclude the advertising. Excellent for learning some new skills and for pointing others in the right direction for their own training.

For my own part, I've learned an enormous amount during my career. It was never a case of starting a new job and being able to instantly carry out every item on the list of duties and responsibilities. I had to learn my way through a range of items from how to reboot my computer in the very early days of Microsoft Windows (when the computers in our office regularly slowed down or froze completely) to how to organise my first conference and how to encourage one of my staff to go on a training course. All of these were new experiences for me and necessitated that I learn something.

I graduated from university in 1991, at a time when there was no internet, no email, no Google ('Almost the age of dinosaurs', you might say!). This meant that whenever I needed to do something I'd never done before, I had to find a way to learn somehow – I couldn't just search on Google for an answer. I learned by asking those around me or, in the case of computing issues, quite often through trial and error (and very regular use of the 'undo' button, something which had been all too missing when I learned to type on an Imperial typewriter during my school years).

In 1995, I started working at a university where we had email and access to a fledgling internet. This was my first experience of connecting with the outside world via computer and I was hooked. It was here that I started to discover the benefits of being able to connect with other people elsewhere in the world and finding out from them how they did things.

During that role, I discovered the usefulness of search engines: one of the professors had held a conference some time before I started working at the university, and she now wanted to get back in touch with all of the speakers to find out how their various projects around the world were progressing, for inclusion in a series of books she was writing. The professor had a handwritten list of names and the universities where they had worked at the time of the conference but nothing more. Making use of my brand new internet skills, I was able to track down all 30 speakers at their universities (including two who had moved on from their roles to other places of learning), and provide her with their email addresses, office phone numbers and postal addresses within just a short time.

Of course, this is now a relatively easy and commonplace task, but at the time my professor was amazed. She had no idea that this sort of information could be found via the internet or any other source at that time, and as a result, in the acknowledgements section of the books which resulted from this work, she proclaimed me as a 'wizard in all forms of technology'.

My internet prowess then led to me being given further research work for her and several of her colleagues at the university, and then I was asked to demonstrate to several other senior secretaries how to do this. Having trained to become a school teacher, but then switching to working in administration as my chosen career, this became my first real experience of delivering a formal training session for adults.

Over the years, the internet has proved to be a fantastic way of networking with and learning from others. My networking began by connecting with PAs and administrators via an intranet within the university, then within a group of universities via a larger network and then with the world at large, and all have assisted me to take on different tasks and different responsibilities.

I've been responsible for teams of staff – some of whom have been very reluctant to learn anything new – so trying to increase their knowledge and skills has been a challenge and a whole new learning experience for me. In one job in particular, I spent a lot of time trying to encourage a secretary (who had flatly refused to use a spreadsheet package) to attend a training course on Microsoft Excel. She fought against this, as she was of the mindset that 'a professional secretary' only typed documents and shouldn't need to work with tables and spreadsheets. After several attempts to cajole her and to appeal to her better judgement, I eventually had to tell her quite frankly that she would be acting extremely unprofessionally if she didn't attend a course that was designed for her professional development. She grumpily went along to the course and, on her return, reported back that she'd had no idea 'a table could be so useful'. I had a very hard time though in getting her to grudgingly admit this. Let's just say that I learned a lot about developing my negotiating skills and working with difficult people in that role!

I have learned something new, almost every day, from every job I've been in. Now that I'm running my own company, I find that there is an enormous amount that I still need to learn – and it's fascinating!

BRAVERY IS ... AIMING
TO BE EXCEPTIONAL IN YOUR ROLE

It's not enough to be good in your job these days.

Firstly, you need to see your role as a career, not just a job. Secondly, you need to aim for something better than good. Competition is extremely fierce: for every good PA out there, there is a large number of better PAs champing at the bit to find a new and challenging role. It makes sense, therefore, to aim to be *exceptional* rather than just good at what you do – like 'brown is the new black', 'exceptional is the new standard'.

But what are the differences between being a good PA and being an exceptional PA?

The PA role is not just secretarial or administrative. It requires skills more closely aligned to those of a senior manager: an accomplished professional with an armoury of talents and a working knowledge of the business that crosses all disciplines. The longer we work for our bosses, the more of their knowledge we take in – after all, without sharing the same knowledge and skills how could we possibly answer their calls, deal with their correspondence, write their reports and keep the school or college running smoothly on their behalf? To be an exceptional PA requires knowledge, qualifications and interaction relevant to that level of expertise, and the ability to soak up that knowledge and use it wisely in supporting our head/principal.

Some of the challenges that can hold us back from achieving excellence are:

- PAs often lack someone to look out for their career development and may not get regular appraisals.
- PAs have to juggle many tasks at once.
- PAs don't often challenge their boss sufficiently because they know how busy the boss is.

- Many PAs don't realise their worth.

To combat this, we should be looking to build:

- More respect for PAs as a profession.
- Increased opportunities and salaries.
- Professional networks and specialist advisers to provide assistance.
- A variety of training courses.
- Strong networking within an exclusive community.

When we stay the same, it's usually not because we haven't made some effort to change. It's usually because we just haven't done anything *today* that could move us towards change.

Think of yourself for a moment as an artist, creating a painting of your potential. If you only think of your painting as a completed masterpiece, an example of reaching the fullest of your potential, then you may be tempted to paint the portrait quickly whilst expecting the result to be of high enough quality to be displayed in an art gallery. If, however, you choose to see the portrait of your potential as a masterpiece-in-progress, then you can feel happier about taking time over each small change, whilst knowing that you are moving in the direction of change – and all the while allowing yourself the opportunity to try out different brush strokes to make small but significant changes to your portrait.

Keep these things in mind as you work towards becoming an exceptional brave PA!

 In 2008, when I applied for the role of principal's PA, I was joined in the application process by 95 others vying for the position. Thankfully, I performed well enough in the interview process to be offered the role. A few months later when we advertised for three receptionist roles, a similar situation occurred – we were inundated with 106 applications. If you are going to apply for a job these days you have to make sure that your application will stand out from the crowd, in order to prove that you, over and above everyone who has applied, are the right person for that job.

BRAVERY IS ... SHOWING COURAGE, COURTESY AND ASPIRATION

Most schools, colleges and universities have a motto – a statement or phrase encapsulating the institution's vision and aims for its students. Most are centred around versions of putting your whole heart into what you are doing, showing integrity or aiming to be the best – or all three.

The motto in the school where I worked was 'Courage, courtesy, aspiration'. The school encouraged the pupils to:

● Have courage in what they did. This was explained to them through the origins of the word, coming from *cor*, the heart. We encouraged them to put their heart into everything they did, to believe in what they were doing and to have faith that their hard work would reap results.

● Show courtesy to others in their interactions. Courtesy related to respecting each other and giving people the space they needed to learn in a safe and nurturing environment, and by encouraging (and expecting) better behaviour from everyone.

● Develop aspiration for their futures. Aspiration was always summed up by one particular slide in the principal's presentation: an image of 10 of our pupils jumping as high as they could, their arms reaching upwards, accompanied by the words, 'Aim for the sky and you will hit the ceiling. Aim for the ceiling and you will fall flat on your bum.' He wanted the pupils to aim as high as they possibly could, and not to limit their hopes and expectations.

If there is one thing that I took away from my time at the school, it was that everyone should bravely reach for the highest they can be.

So, if courage, courtesy and aspiration are attributes we want our students to live, work and learn by, how can we also reflect this in our own working practices as PAs?

You could concentrate on:

HAVING COURAGE IN WHAT YOU DO

- Sticking to your guns when you know something is right.
- Trying out new methods of doing things.
- Not being afraid to try and fail.
- Believing in your own skills and expertise,
- Not being content to settle for being thought of as 'just a PA'.
- Pushing for recognition for your role and skills.

SHOWING COURTESY TO OTHERS IN YOUR INTERACTIONS

- Maintaining a calm, polite and professional manner (as much as possible!).
- When confronted with a heated situation, remembering that the other person has probably had a bad day, so don't take what they say personally.
- Giving others room to do what they need to – be generous with your time and space.
- Showing that when you are listening to someone, you are fully hearing what is being said.
- Remembering that politeness, good manners and a smile can go a long way.

BEING ASPIRATIONAL

- Being a mentor/coach for other members of your admin team.
- Delegating tasks to others that will challenge them to learn further and show that you believe in them (rather than only ever giving them something which you know they can pretty much do with their eyes closed).
- Keeping your own standards high and expecting similar from others.
- Setting a great example for others to aspire towards.
- Aspiring to reach something better for yourself.

So, when did you last display some courage, courtesy and aspiration?

BRAVERY IS ... ADMITTING '1 DON'T KNOW' OR '1 HAVE TRIED AND FAILED'

Being a great PA means being OK with admitting that you don't know something and asking for help, or finding things out for yourself when help isn't available, rather than just sitting around saying, 'It can't be done – I don't know how.'

Not only do you need to be brave enough to admit it when you don't know something, and that you need someone else's assistance, but also humble enough to put your hand in the air and admit it when you have made a mistake. This will mean a lot to those you work with – they will recognise that, whilst they may see you as some kind of Superwoman/Superman/Super-PA, you are actually human and do get things wrong sometimes. It is crucial to admit to having this human side – we can all too often put forward the view of being indestructible or invincible, purely because we are the one person to whom everyone else turns for help. So, if you have done something wrong, or tried something that didn't work, or made something worse by attempting the wrong fix, always be ready to admit to it.

Most mistakes are forgivable and even salvageable, but there are five things you should try your absolute hardest *not* to do in your role in education:

1. Never speak, behave or quit out of rage or revenge. Words can be twisted by others, emails can be read in a different 'tone of voice' than the one you intended to use, and people can take offence at written or spoken words all too easily. And once said and done, it's very hard to take things back.

2. Never backstab your colleagues – it will invariably bite you in the behind. Don't attempt to play one colleague off against another or assume that things you say about someone behind their back will not make their way to them. People talk. Gossips spread rumours.

3. Never lie to avoid facing the consequences of the truth – again, karma will get you. Don't try to pass the blame on to someone else or claim that you didn't know what was happening if you actually did. What possible further working relationships can you build with your head teacher or colleagues if you lie to them?

4. Never proclaim that you are miserable in your job. If you hate what you do, get out. Complaining but staying put will push your colleagues towards disliking you. Why should they put the effort in to work hard to build a working relationship with you if you are only going to moan about how much you dislike your job?

5. Never burn bridges with your colleagues – you need to work together! If you have a disagreement with someone, resolve it as best you can. If that means you need to make an apology or put forward the olive branch of friendship in order to rebuild things, do it. Don't hold a grudge, and don't do anything that would drastically prevent you from working together as a team.

No matter how long you have been in your role, there will always be some things you don't know or mistakes that can be made. Admitting to that deficit and then, most importantly, doing something about it, is the best thing you can do. And if someone tells you that they don't know how to do something, or that they have tried and failed, then help them out as best you can. Don't laugh or sneer – if you can show them how, do so. You never know when you might need that same level of help from them or someone else.

We learn by failing and trying again. If you want an example of this, watch a baby in its first attempts to stand up. They will pull themselves up and then fall, again and again, until they finally get it right and manage to stay upright. But if every time they try to stand up their mother picks them up and puts them back into their bed and tucks the covers tightly around them to stop them from trying again, they will eventually give up.

Don't give up trying in your role, no matter what. And don't be afraid to admit you don't know something or need help.

BRAVERY IS ... UNDERSTANDING YOU'RE NOT 'TOO GOOD' TO MAKE TEA AND COFFEE

It is *not* beneath you to make tea or coffee. It *should* be beneath you, however, to mess up a drinks order!

It is your role as a personal assistant, executive assistant, secretary, senior secretary, whatever you call yourself, to assist your head and support them in whatever way is necessary to enable them to carry out their role successfully.

In order to assist them in meetings with other staff, VIPs, visitors, directors, governors or parents, you may be called on to make tea and coffee or to organise for refreshments to be brought in. If you have a catering facility in your school or college, check with them (or with your finance department) to find out whether it would be most cost-effective to get them to service all your meetings or whether it might work out cheaper to have a small coffee/tea-making machine installed either in or near your office, expressly for the purpose of serving your head, the leadership team and their meetings.

If it's going to cost a large amount of money for catering staff to make pots of coffee and tea, and then bring them through the school building, up two flights of stairs to your office, by which time the drinks will be half cold, it may be more economical for you to make the drinks yourself in your own area. However, if this means that the world and its brother (i.e. the rest of the school staff) are then going to be hanging around your office (and subsequently your drinks machine) like a pack of thirsty dogs in the midday sun, you might want to think about how and to whom you restrict the use of the drinks machine, or charge for supplies!

SO ... THERE'S A MEETING HAPPENING LATER TODAY. WHO'S HAVING WHAT?

Start to keep a spreadsheet, chart or notebook detailing who drinks what, so if there is a meeting happening later today you will already know what needs to be prepared. You could store the information in Outlook against individuals' contact details, log the details alphabetically in an address book or create a mini-spreadsheet detailing everyone's varying requirements (whether they prefer tea or coffee, caffeinated vs. decaffeinated, whether they take milk, sugar, sweeteners, etc.). Yes, I hear you yelling 'Geek!' at me right now, but I do have a point!

You will impress the governors, sponsors or people who haven't visited for over a year no end if, when they enter the office, you can greet them and say correctly, 'You like your coffee with milk and two sugars, right?' It's one of those little things that shows you have paid attention and that you care. It also demonstrates that you are acting professionally in trying to ensure that everyone receives a good welcome and takes away a positive image of the school or college.

In addition to earning you special brownie points for knowing what they like and what they don't like, it will save you time. You won't have to try to remember it all in a mental note (or scribble it on a notepad). Once the drinks are made, a simple method for remembering whose drink is whose is to arrange the drinks alphabetically on a tray to carry them in, ready to distribute to the right people – remembering that A is at top left on the tray and working round clockwise. Then walk into the room, put down the tray and hand the correct drinks to the correct people without a word. They will think you're a memory marvel!

Example:

Amy – tea, milk, 1 sugar

Debra – coffee, milk, 2 sugars

Phyllis – tea, milk

John – coffee, black

Matt – green tea

There are a few other issues that you should bear in mind when wearing your barista's hat:

- Mopping up. When it comes to the logistics of dealing with dirty cups, make sure you keep a tray to hand so that you can clear the boss's office as soon as possible after a meeting. They are not going to want the previous meeting's cups still to be hanging around when starting the next meeting.

- To teacup or not to teacup, that is the question! Does your manager have a particular preference for a teacup, mug or plastic cup? Do you have certain visitors who warrant the best china, with a milk jug, spoons and sugar bowl, or does everyone get the same old same old polystyrene/plastic cup?

- Washing up. If you have a dishwasher on site, try to make arrangements with someone in the catering staff to collect dirty cups from your room and return clean ones to you on a daily basis.

- Always, always, always have a supply of napkins or paper towels on hand. Someone will invariably spill their drink, and it will always be when you are busily engaged on something else, so make sure the mop-up tissues are stored somewhere easily accessible.

- Additional must-haves. Make sure you have supplies of spoons, spare cups, bottled water and glasses – after reeling out the many different options available from your drinks machine ('Breakfast tea, Earl Grey, peppermint, green, decaf …?'), there will always be someone who asks for a glass of water or some hot water because they drink it on its own or carry their own supply of herbal teabags.

- Food and plates. Sandwich lunches, biscuits or fruit may be required for some meetings. If you are using decent cups, it makes sense to have a set of matching plates and bowls too, or at least have access to them from the kitchens at short notice.

BRAVERY IS ... ENCOURAGING PAs TO MEET AND NETWORK

Far too often, the role of a PA is an isolated one. We live and breathe at our desks; our office walls are the boundaries of our working world. It is important to be able to peer over the edge of the desk and encounter a world of others in parallel roles who we can learn from and who can learn from us. There are PAs, EAs, secretaries and other administrators out there who are experiencing similar frustrations, similar highs and lows, similar challenges and similar experiences.

Networking with other PAs and EAs allows you to reach out and connect with them, to share knowledge, expertise, learning, irritations and delights. Share the wealth of your knowledge and expertise, not just with other administrators within your own school or college, but with others in the same field elsewhere.

If there isn't a ready-made network for you to join locally, you might consider setting up your own for PAs and administrators working in the schools or colleges in your city or an internal network within your university. You will undoubtedly have contact details for a lot of other PAs out there from your communications with their offices on behalf of your head teacher/principal. Send out invitations to an afternoon or evening meeting where you can introduce yourselves, discuss training needs and perhaps offer to help each other.

In the UK, there are digital networks such as the Specialist Schools and Academies Trust's (SSAT – www.ssat.co.uk) network for PAs in academies and an equivalent network for PAs in schools. There is also the National Association of Head Teachers' PAs network (www.nahpa.org.uk), plus networking discussion groups on LinkedIn. These are great places where you can learn from and share knowledge and expertise with fellow PAs in educational institutions.

You may well meet naysayers who claim that there is no worth in networking. However, more and more head teachers are joining email discussion groups and/or LinkedIn groups, and sharing their knowledge and expertise. Most heads regularly meet with the heads of other schools in the local area. If you want to know more about what you could get out of being in a network, ask your head teacher what they get from theirs!

Networking can be immensely useful for PAs. Sometimes, just knowing that there is someone else out there who has experienced something similar to what you might be going through, and who you could ask for help, advice or a listening ear, can be enough, without even having to call on them for their assistance. Being able to meet up with them on a semi-regular basis, or being able to reach them by phone or email, can make all the difference between being given an almost insurmountable task and completing it successfully, because you have drawn on the experience of someone else with the know-how.

Your network should aim to have a termly meeting to discuss continuing professional development (CPD) items in person, so that you can further yourselves in your careers. You will probably find it hard work to get PAs to attend these meetings – everyone will be 'too busy', or it will be 'too far', or it won't be seen as 'important enough' – but please keep prompting them to make time to attend. As soon as they have attended a meeting with other PAs, they will begin to see how useful it can be – especially when they start to put names to the faces of their peers from other schools or colleges – and will be keen to come along again in the future. The best way for us all to become great in our jobs is to share our knowledge, to learn from each other, to develop each other's skills and to build on our knowledge collectively.

Some of the most influential networking places for PAs include:

- **www.linkedin.com** – Register for free and connect with business people worldwide or just in your area or country. Quite apart from building a network of contacts all around the world, you might choose to join one or two of the thousands of discussion groups on the site and share the wealth of your knowledge with others. Within a group, any member can post a question as a new discussion item – or respond to anyone else's discussion – and they can be an absolute mine of information. Jump into a discussion and participate!

- **www.euma.org** – European Management Assistants (EUMA) was founded in 1974 and is currently represented in 26 countries. It is the only European management assistants' association that offers its members access to a professional network encompassing a vast range of business cultures, languages and lifestyles, whilst at the same time it is a network where everyone is on common ground and among friends. EUMA also looks outwards and has links with other international management assistant associations, such as the International Association of Administrative Professionals (IAAP) in the United States.

- **www.deskdemon.com** – Launched in the UK in August 2000, DeskDemon works with PAs, office managers, secretaries and admin staff, along with the UK's professional secretarial associations, to deliver a single website encompassing all aspects of office management.

● **www.pa-assist.com** – A great portal site providing resources, services and assistance to make your job easier. You can also sign up for the free monthly newsletter.

For more information on networking, including how to build your initial network, see the Resources section at the end of the book.

 I'm a prolific networker, and since 2009 I've been the 'most connected PA on the planet', as one networking colleague calls me. On LinkedIn I'm connected at first level to over 21,000 people, and I have the largest network of any personal assistant, executive assistant, admin and trainer of PAs, plus the 'PAs, EAs, VAs and Senior Administrators' group that I created is nearing 70,000 members. Networking has led to a 'real job' which includes me doing two things I would never have dreamed of before: collecting frequent flyer miles whilst working with some of the most amazing PAs in the world!

Of course, building an absolutely massive network isn't for everybody. But networking on any scale can have huge importance for you because it opens your mind to new possibilities by connecting and sharing with professionals in similar roles elsewhere.

BRAVERY IS ... DISCOVERING
DIFFERENT WAYS TO SAVE
TIME ON TASKS

A major prerequisite for the role of PA is to be able to manage time. This doesn't mean you need a degree in Einsteinian physics and an ability to either bend time or time-travel (although most PAs would agree that this would be a very useful thing to be able to do!), but you need to be able to keep a check on how long things take you to do, how much you can get done in a particular timeframe and to plan/schedule your time to make best use of the hours available to you. You also need to be able to plan your manager's time. Actually, that physics degree might be quite useful, after all!

So, it pays to have a number of time-saving techniques at your fingertips. In this chapter we'll look at just a few, including schedules for email, utilising whatever resources are available to you to gather tips from others, planning your week effectively, scheduling difficult tasks, accepting good enough over perfection and knowing what your time is worth.

SETTING UP A SYSTEM FOR DEALING
WITH EMAILS AND MESSAGES

In all PA roles you will need to set up some sort of system for dealing with your incoming emails. The basics for this could include:

- Establish a schedule for when you will check your email. This means not checking your email all day long and not being disturbed by messages arriving all the time. Turn off the auto-notification (the little 'ping' noise and envelope icon that pops up in the corner of your screen to alert you to new mail). Instead, set appointments on your calendar to check your email four or five times a day – for example, first thing in the morning, mid-morning, straight after lunch, mid-afternoon and before the end of the day.

- Create folders in your school or college's email system to store your emails. Basic folders could include: urgent items for action, non-urgent important items, ICT, finance, projects (by name), departments (by name), meetings and papers, etc.

- If you use Outlook, make use of the 'categories' function to easily colour-code emails. This allows you to organise the emails in your inbox by category.

- Develop your own methods (using mail filters, flagging, automatic highlights, etc.) to 'flag' urgent emails so they are easy to find in your inbox.

- As soon as you have finished dealing with an email, move it (and other related emails if it's a conversation thread) out of your inbox into one of your filing folders. In this way, you know that anything left in your inbox still needs your attention.

USING INDUSTRY-RELATED PUBLICATIONS AND RESOURCES TO HELP YOU SAVE TIME IN YOUR ROLE

There are some fantastic resources out there to help you to save time in your work. Some of these may come from your colleagues or other PAs in other schools and colleges, and a large number can be found in PA magazines, books and websites, as well as your own tried and tested devices. Spending half an hour of your week reading about or researching the latest trends could well save you a lot more time during the weeks that follow. (See the Resources section for some details of magazines, books and websites.)

When you meet with other PAs at networking events or conferences, you might start by asking them about their time-saving tips, then after the event share all the tips with those present (making sure to give credit to the originators of ideas – and gaining their permission to share them!).

SOME KEY PRINCIPLES FOR PLANNING A DAY OR A WEEK EFFECTIVELY

- Keep an up-to-date list of everything that you currently have to do (your action list).

- Find 30 minutes at the same time every week to plan your week – identifying key priorities.

- Use your diary to set aside time to complete activities and for admin tasks (e.g. reviewing your in-tray, making calls, going through the day's post, filing, managing emails, meeting preparation, planning).

- Review your diary and your action list every morning to establish your priorities for the day. Write them on one page of A4 paper and keep it on your desk. If you do nothing else today, do these and you will have had a good day!

- When setting up your day's schedule each morning, make sure that you add anything left over from yesterday's action list.

- Always be ready to review your schedule: as priorities change or other urgent tasks come in during the week, be prepared to adapt and be flexible.

- Rather than just write on your weekly schedule the name of a large task or project and expect to complete it during the week, break it down into smaller parts that can be completed on a day-to-day basis, then add these into your daily schedules. It is a useful mind-trick: you will find it so much more satisfying to acknowledge at the end of the day that you have completed several items on your daily list, rather than feeling that you are only part-way through something much larger.

- Create a daily time schedule and try to stick to it.

SOME TIPS FOR SCHEDULING DIFFICULT, NON-URGENT, LARGE OR DULL TASKS

- Get the worst tasks over with as soon as you can each day. Think of it as a BHT (Big Horrible Task) and get it done. Imagine your BHT is that you have to eat a frog or a bucket of worms each day (you absolutely *have* to). If you put it off until later in the day, you will spend all of your time during the day dreading the BHT, but if you just do it first thing and get it over with, you can then spend the rest of your day doing everything else quite happily.

- Are you a paper-shuffler (in other words, you pick up a piece of paper with details of a task on it, read it, procrastinate about doing it and put it down again, only to pick it up again later in the day or tomorrow – and it takes many more pick-ups until you actually get around to doing it)? If this sounds like you, every time you pick it up, bite off a corner of the page. The aim here is to change the way you do things, and to stop procrastinating so that you knuckle down and get the task done before you eat the whole page!

- Pair a treat with a dull task – 'I'll finish this, then I'll have a cup of tea.'

- For big tasks, break things down into smaller tasks and take on one a day. Liken it to the worms: you can't swallow an entire bucket of worms in one mouthful. Break it down to one gulp at a time.

- Act sooner rather than later. An important but non-urgent task can become urgent if you keep putting it off every day.

- Try to tackle at least five important tasks daily, including simple tasks like phone calls that are essential for moving a project along.

- Include 'sequential' and 'simultaneous' tasks in your schedule, so that you can save even more time. Find tasks that you can do in sequence which allow you to keep your brain fired up in the same mindset for each one (e.g. if you handle both your principal's and the chair of governor's expense claims each month, schedule to do them both on the same morning) and those which you can do whilst other tasks are completing (e.g. whilst printing a large document on your office printer you could go and get your photocopying done).

FOR SOME TASKS, 'GOOD ENOUGH' WILL DO

It pays to manage your time well, because it's a fact that managing your time well makes you successful. Good time management can help to level the playing field between natural winners and the rest of mankind. A good strategy is to remind yourself that for busy office professionals, doing things perfectly is less valuable to your organisation than doing things adequately.

Doing things adequately will allow sufficient time in your time budget to stay on top of important projects and meet important deadlines. It's tempting to reword that paragraph in your email one more time before hitting the send button, because you love to write and want to get it word perfect, but good enough will do.

This does not negate the advice of always striving to be an exceptional PA. By performing a task to a good enough capacity, and then moving on to other tasks and responsibilities, you will be providing your head teacher or principal with a far better service than concentrating too much of your efforts on perfecting just one task.

IT HELPS TO KNOW WHAT YOU ARE WORTH!

If you aren't sure whether you are spending too long on a piece of work, or if it should be done at all, calculate how much your time is worth (i.e. your salary divided by X weeks, then divided by Y hours per week), and record how you spend your time, hour by hour, over a week on a particular project. Knowing the value of your time should help you to allocate your time effectively. This is also a useful technique to use with your boss if their diary is too full of meetings. Ask them, 'Are there any meetings that are not actually good value for money for you to attend at your salary? Might it be better to send another member of the leadership team instead?'

Don't just be content to continue doing things in the same way as you have always done, or following the timelines of your predecessors. Bravely find your own ways to manage your time, and if you find a technique for something that really works for you, share it with your colleagues, pass it on to other PAs in your network or blog about it on LinkedIn. Share the wealth of your expertise and experience to help others to manage their time as well as you do.

BRAVERY IS ... BLOWING A TRUMPET FOR MODERN PAS AND REFUSING TO BE A STEREOTYPICAL 1950S SECRETARY

OK. It's PA Question Time! How much do you know about the PA community and are you a good ambassador?

- Did you know that 2014 was (a) the International Year of the Secretary and Administrator (IYOTSA 2014), and (b) the 30th anniversary of the first Year of the Secretary in the USA in 1984?

- Do you know the titles of and subscribe to any PA magazines or educational newspapers, and do you actually read them?

- Do you attend at least one PA-related event each year (e.g. Confex, the Office show, a networking group for PAs from any industry, a schools PA network)?

- Do you know when the UK's National PA Day is?[1]

---

1 IYOTSA 2014 was led by the team at the Professional Association for Secretaries and Administrators (PAFSA), based in South Africa. Preparations for the year of celebrations throughout 2014 started in 2010, and involved hundreds of PA associations worldwide. Details are on the PAFSA website: www.pafsa.co.za. Information about PA-related magazines, events such as Confex and Office and PA networks are included in the Resources section at the back of this book.

The UK's National PA Day is a moveable feast, celebrated in October each year on one of the two days of the Office show. Visit www.officeshow.co.uk to find out more.

⊛ Have you done anything within your school, college or
university to promote the power of the PA in the workplace?

⊛ Do you cringe if someone refers to you as 'just a PA' or 'just a
secretary'?

⊛ Are you proud of your job and of what you do, and of what you
have achieved in the time you have been there?

If you answered 'yes' to most or all of these questions, hurrah, you
are already a role model for the PA profession. If your answer to any
of these questions is 'no', then shame on you – you and I need to
have a few words!

Part of your role as PA will undoubtedly be to serve as an ambassador
for your school or college, especially in the absence of your head
teacher or principal. You should be proud to talk to visitors and
guests about the institution and what you are all collectively
working towards. You should aim to extend this to include being an
ambassador for the PA profession too.

Too many people over the years have dismissed the roles of
PAs, secretaries and administrators as unimportant, as 'just an
administrator', 'just a secretary', just this, just that. We need to
change this mindset – after all, approximately a quarter of the world's
working population are employed in administrative roles, and the
PA/EA/secretarial role is the most important administrative role of
all, as we are the people supporting the leaders of our organisations.

Films, books and TV programmes tend to portray secretaries in
three characteristically stereotypical ways. Apparently, we are mute
bimbos sitting bored at a desk, polishing our nails and wearily
taking phone messages. Or we are pitched to the world as demure,
terrified of authority, nervous, quiet, downtrodden and mouse-like,
almost pathologically efficient at typing letters and only ever speak
when spoken to – the quiet, timid 'Miss Jones' secretary from the
1950s. Or we are sexy vixens intent on seducing the photocopier
repair man (if you type in the word 'secretary' or 'assistant' into the
book search pages on Amazon, there are a phenomenal number of
romantic or racy novels based on the ridiculously stereotyped image
of the sex-starved secretary!).

These stereotypes do us a huge disservice. We need to change people's views of who we are and what we do. We need to strive for recognition of the role of personal assistant as a genuine profession.

In terms of blowing your own trumpet about what *you* do in your school or college, do remember that there is a massive difference between 'showing off' and telling someone that you have done something that you are really proud of. There should be great credit in using an achievement to encourage a fellow staff member or a pupil to change their mindset about working in a PA role.

There are several PA of the Year competitions/awards schemes out there, and more are added each year. Why not get your boss to nominate you? Please don't feel that you can't do this. You can, and you should.

Why? Well, if you are proud of what you do at your school/college and you know your head or principal is also happy with your work, then they should be nominating you. However, it is very unlikely that your head or principal reads any of the PA-related websites or publications which sponsor these awards, so it's only by bringing them to their attention that you are likely to be nominated, so put an award nomination form in front of them!

As a starter list, look online for details (and closing dates for nominations) for:

- Executive PA/Hays PA of the Year – **www.executivepa.com**
- Secs in the City PA of the Year – **www.secsinthecity. co.uk**
- Pitman Training Super Achievers Awards – superachievers.pitman-training.com
- EUMA PA of the Year – **www.euma.org**
- London PA of the Year – **www.londonlaunch.com**

A number of colleagues who saw my award certificates asked what I had done that warranted being nominated and shortlisted for an award, so I told them about the various tasks for which I was nominated. From their reactions, it was quite clear that they had absolutely no idea that I was responsible for those tasks, and they didn't actually have much of a clue as to what I did in my job for the rest of the working week!

When you are nominated for an award, be proud to put the details on display and tell your colleagues and the students about it. Whilst it's sad to realise that many people know so little about the PA role, it should be our duty to educate those around us about what a PA actually does, and to push for recognition of such a professional role.

So relish your successes – for example, you might write an article and submit it to a PA magazine. When it is published, share it with others. If you attend a training course, or you find a great website full of valuable tips, utilise what you have learned within your job. If this saves you time in your job, then pass the learning on to other administrators in your school, and share with them the source of the information so that they can do some researching of their own. Talk with the pupils at your school or the students at your college or university, and ask them what they know about your role – you never know, you might encourage and inspire somebody to become a PA!

Celebrate being good at what you do, and knowing that others appreciate your efforts. There are many things you could do in order to be an ambassador for the PA profession.

What did I do to be an ambassador for PAs and for my school? The short answer is: everything I possibly could!

 During my career I have been nominated (and shortlisted) for Secretary of the Year, Head Teacher's PA of the Year and PA of the Year, and each time I put the certificates on display in my office. This was not to say, 'La, la, la, look at me, aren't I wonderful?' but to educate those around me that the role of PA is something to be celebrated.

I have been writing for PA magazines and delivering training and networking events for PAs since 2010. I have also chaired several networking groups for PAs, including the SSAT PA network across all of the UK's academies. Throughout, I've been campaigning for recognition for the role of personal assistant and executive assistant.

Everything I did in my role as the principal's PA was done on behalf of the school, endeavouring to make sure that I gave as positive a welcome to our visitors as possible and to ensure that they went away knowing what the school was about, our vision, our ethos, what we were trying to do for the pupils and the local area. I evangelised to them about what our principal was doing, how he inspired the staff and the pupils to reach for the stars, how he encouraged all of us to be the best that we could be, and how we were making huge in-roads in changing the educational experiences (and therefore the futures) of our pupils.

And why wouldn't I? It was in the best job of my life and I truly loved it. I felt incredibly inspired by my boss and how he saw the future of education for our pupils, and I made sure that anyone visiting the school went away with this positive feeling. If guests came to my office, of course, I gave them the obligatory visitors' pack (school prospectus, pen, memory stick, copy of the latest newsletter, etc.), but if they were waiting for a few minutes to meet the principal I didn't leave them sitting on a chair in my office to wait. I gave them some information about the school and the latest projects or ventures that our pupils were taking part in.

When undergraduate students came to my office to complete their police check and DBS application forms, I shared my enthusiasm for what we were doing. I told them of the changes we had made (from what happened at the predecessor school to our new ways in the academy), and I told them about the effect these changes were having on our pupils – which the pupils and their parents had reported back on. I told them of the rising expectations amongst the local community that our pupils were going to go on to better things, and that some of them were even starting to talk about their chances of getting into university in the future.

As an ambassador for the school, there was no way on earth that I could have fulfilled this role as a quiet 1950s mouse of a figure.

BRAVERY IS ... BRACING
YOURSELF FOR NEW CHALLENGES AND DARING TO DO SOMETHING DIFFERENTLY

Don't be afraid to try new things. They might scare the heck out you, but it can often feel far better to have had a go than to spend the next few weeks or months wondering, 'I wonder what might have happened if ...'

If whatever you try goes wrong, at least you tried. As a great PA, I'm sure there will be a way that you can find out how to fix whatever it is or locate someone who can fix it for you. And if whatever you try goes right, hurrah!

Sometimes it might be a small 'something' that challenges us, sometimes it might be an enormous task. Either way, if you can try to embrace the challenge with enthusiasm and determination, knowing that you have lots of skills that can help you to succeed, then success will often find its way to you. If, however, you go into it thinking, 'This is all going to go wrong,' then guess what? You may well be right.

Each and every one of us in a PA role has our own huge range of internalised skills and expertise that we can draw on, and now that networking is so easy – via websites such as LinkedIn where we can ask questions of our PA peers worldwide – we also have access to even more resources to build on.

So, what sort of out-of-the-ordinary tasks, challenges or new opportunities might you get involved in to further your own role and to help your fellow members of the PA community?

JOINING, SETTING UP OR CHAIRING A NETWORK

We've already looked at the benefits of networking with other PAs (see page 51), which can provide a huge boost to your professional development. Is there a localised network of PAs near you that you could join? If there isn't, could you consider creating one? You will invariably have contact names for PAs working in other schools nearby (and if you haven't, you should be able to find them out relatively easily). Start by sending some emails or making some phone calls to start bringing a group together.

CONTRIBUTING TO A PA-RELATED MAGAZINE OR WEBSITE

I'm willing to bet there is something in your repertoire of PA skills that you could impart to others. If you've got good writing skills, why not put pen to paper (or fingertip to keyboard) and write an article or short piece about that skill and submit it to a PA magazine or website? If you can provide a photo or two that is relevant to the piece, even better. (Don't worry if you haven't because editors can find appropriate images to match articles if required.)

Now, before you say, 'Oh, I couldn't do that,' why *wouldn't* you be able to do that? You write reports and letters, you draft newsletters and school publications, you probably have a hand in creating the marketing materials for your school or college, so why wouldn't you be skilled enough to write a few hundred words about an aspect of your job, something that you know so much about? Check the Resources section for details of some PA magazines and websites.

OFFERING TRAINING TO YOUR ADMIN COLLEAGUES AND FELLOW PAs

Are you the school expert on using Excel? Are you great at designing posters and brochures for college productions? Have you got relevant skills in something that you could share with your colleagues in the administrative team or with fellow PAs at a networking event?

One really simple thing you could do would be to set up a half-hour session once a month or once a fortnight for your colleagues offering to show them certain aspects of how to use Word, Excel, Outlook or another package used in your school. Encourage other administrative colleagues to also put themselves forward for delivering a session or two. Make it as informal as you like, with tea and biscuits as enticements to attend, but do it! Don't be the one and only person in your organisation who can do a certain task in a certain way using a certain piece of software – what will they do if you break a leg and can't come into work for a few weeks? Share your knowledge and expertise! We'll come back to this scenario later in the book when I advise you to start listing your regular major tasks in your purple folder (see page 117) to help out in the event of you being absent, but make sure you show someone how to do those tasks, or at least provide some pointers on how to start!

You might be nervous about the idea of presenting some learning to your colleagues. Try not to worry – it's quite normal to feel apprehensive about something like this. It might mean that you need to give your little bag of bravery a shake to find the courage to stand up in front of your colleagues; if so, sit down and do it instead! Make it feel like an ordinary meeting and don't be unnecessarily hard on yourself.

Take some time beforehand to prepare what you are going to demonstrate and what you are going to say. You might want to do a basic presentation or use an interactive whiteboard (if your school/ college has one), so that you can sit at a laptop and demonstrate on a large screen.

If you are nervous, a technique that might help is to split the planning process into two parts. First, pretend that someone else will be doing the presenting and let yourself get on with the task of creating the presentation, without worrying constantly that you have to find the courage to present it. Next, when the presentation is ready, concentrate on practising and gaining some confidence in how to present it, safe in the knowledge that the presentation itself is well planned. The better the planning, the lesser the panic.

When you realise that the topic you are going to be talking about is something that you do on a regular basis, you should find it easier to put aside some of the fear of speaking in front of others. You will hopefully surprise yourself by finding a little nugget of courage in your bravery bag, secure in the knowledge that you understand very well what you are going to be talking about.

 On a personal note, one of my most recent challenges that I had to find some bravery for was overcoming ill health and daring to think about making some huge decisions about my future career. For the last two years that I worked at the academy, I suffered from ill health, which required a whole lot of bravery all of its own, going through five surgical procedures plus blood transfusions and generally feeling unwell for a long time.

After my last surgery and a long period of sick leave, it became apparent that my health was not good enough to return to work full-time. Much as I loved my five-and-a-half years in post as the principal's PA, I made the decision to leave for the sake of my health. This then gave me the space and time to concentrate on making plans to deliver training courses on a part-time basis for PAs, EAs and administrators.

This was quite possibly one of the hardest moves of my career, requiring a good shake of my bravery bag to find the courage (and daring) to leave a secure, pensioned, full-time permanent job in education and go it alone with my training business. But it was definitely the right decision for me:

it was something completely new, and I found a way to embrace the new challenges it brought.

BRAVERY IS ... BOUNCING IDEAS OFF SOMEONE ELSE – AND BEING A BOUNCER YOURSELF!

If you have a great idea – perhaps something that might make your work easier, help a colleague, save the school or college some money or an improvement to an existing procedure – don't just keep it to yourself. It might feel daunting to put an idea forward to your boss or another colleague, but nothing ventured, nothing gained!

Sometimes you just need to be brave and speak up. However, there are some steps you can take to help you to do this in a professional way. It's not just a case of pushing open your boss's door, blurting out your idea and running for the hills!

Preparation, you will find, is everything. Before presenting your idea, you should first go through it thoroughly, looking at the *who, what, when, where, why* and *how*. This will give you the best opportunity to demonstrate your idea in the best light.

WHO DO YOU SPEAK TO?

It may be that, depending on your idea, your boss might not be the best person to talk to about it. If, for example, you work in the HR department, but you have an idea about financial transactions, then it might be better for you to speak to someone in the finance department rather than the HR director. Use your common sense to decide who is the most appropriate person to speak to about your idea.

WHAT BENEFITS COULD YOUR IDEA BRING?

Once you have decided on the most appropriate person to speak with, think about what your idea could bring to the school/college. Process your thoughts. Think about the pros and cons of your idea, consider the various advantages and expand on them. Try to cover each angle, including the negative points, so that you will be less likely to be shot down prematurely. If you can show that you have already considered the negative points, they are more likely to listen to the positive points.

WHEN IS THE BEST TIME TO PITCH YOUR IDEA?

There will certainly be bad times to pitch your idea to someone, so try to identify the best time – not only the right time of day and the right day of the week, but the appropriate point within the school/college year. After all, it's probably not the best of timing to be putting forward a fantastic idea for next year's Christmas show just a few weeks into the January term – you would probably get a much better response if you pitched your idea in September, before the preparations start for the next show. Similarly, if your idea is going to involve a large budget, the best time to present it might be early in the next financial year when you can put in a timely bid for funding.

WHERE DO YOU PRESENT YOUR IDEA?

If you want a serious conversation about your idea, then the environment must be right too. Putting an idea forward to your head teacher or principal whilst you are walking with them through the building is not the right environment and is unlikely to result in the best response. You need to take your idea seriously and give it the appropriate space. Opt for a formal setting, such as booking a meeting into your head teacher's diary and presenting your idea to them in their office or in a meeting room.

WHY SHOULD YOUR IDEA BE APPROVED?

Go back to the benefits of your idea and identify any potential problems with carrying it through. Are there any reasons why your idea *shouldn't* be approved? Develop solutions to these problems and identify who would be affected at each stage of your plan. If you can show that you have really thought your idea through, and have looked into the various pitfalls as well as the benefits, the greater the chance of your idea being accepted.

HOW DO OTHERS FEEL ABOUT YOUR IDEA?

If you aren't sure that the person you are going to speak to will give a full listening ear to your idea, or you don't feel that you are the type to take the initiative, try out your idea on a few colleagues to gauge their responses. Knowing that others are behind your idea may give you the impetus to put it forward in a confident manner. Your toughest critics are likely to be the people you work with, so if they are excited by your idea, try to carry that excitement through with you into the pitch!

Once your idea is approved, implemented and becomes reality, give yourself a pat on the back. Share this congratulatory pat with anyone else who was involved in making it happen, and make sure that you make a note of this successful idea and implementation so that you can bring it up at your next performance review or job interview.

You can also use this system of questions with anyone who comes to you to sound out their own ideas. Ask them to look at the who, what, when, where, why and how in order to help them pitch their ideas in the best way possible.

BRAVERY IS ... HOLDING BACK THE URGE TO MURDER YOUR COLLEAGUES AT CHRISTMAS!

As a PA you need to be a fantastic organiser. This is a great skill and something to be highly commended. However, being the school/college/university 'expert' on organising meetings may earn you one of the unseen 'benefits' of being great at your job: you may be asked to arrange the staff Christmas party or Secret Santa.

To some PAs I've met, just the words 'Christmas party' and 'Secret Santa' can strike a chord of horror. Not because either task is a horrible one but because it can be so difficult to try to please everybody all of the time.

Please don't get me wrong: both celebrations are lovely sentiments – gathering people together at Christmas and showing each other that you care – but over the years I have found that they can be two of the most frustrating tasks you come up against. Countless other PAs around the world agree on this whenever the topics come up at training events. We all love the *idea* of everyone getting together for a lovely Christmas party and of giving each other gifts to celebrate Christmas, but it can be incredibly hard to pull it off without losing more than a little patience and goodwill.

If you are a new PA and haven't yet experienced either event from the organisational side of things, you are probably thinking, 'What's so bad about organising the staff Christmas party?' Well, let's see ...

- No one can agree on a venue. Someone will always moan that they don't like it, but nobody wants to take the task off your hands.

- No one can agree on what night of the week it should take place – certainly not a weekend night because weekends are sacrosanct, but if it's during the week will anyone be fit for work the next day (because the younger staff are determined to get very drunk)?

- Julie says she will attend the party but doesn't want to sit near anyone from her department (she *does* like them, you understand, she just thinks she really ought to be socialising with other people).

- Sandra won't have the meal, thank you, but she will sit at a table sipping cocktails and glaring at the waiters all night (they are confused by her presence and keep trying to offer her food – don't they know she's on a diet?).

- Several staff will have dietary requirements which are usually manageable, except there will always be at least one person with the most difficult needs (think of a gluten-free, fruit-free *and* nut-allergic vegan), who will demand having a version of Christmas pudding produced exclusively for them, then moan that it was inedible.

- The younger teaching staff won't want a sit-down meal, they'll just want to go to the pub for the evening; the older staff want a meal, but don't want to go to the pub.

- The lower paid staff won't want to go to X as it's too expensive; the higher paid staff don't want to go to Y as it's too low-brow for their tastes.

- Three people won't turn up on the night, and someone else will bring an uninvited guest. Somebody else won't have paid their deposit but will turn up regardless and sneak on to a table thinking it's funny to be getting a 'free' evening out. You will spend the evening fuming at their bare-faced cheek and rudeness but, of course, you can't bring it up, because it's a party and we're all meant to be having a lovely time.

- Someone will bring their objectionable, opinionated, highly critical and/or very boring partner along and will proceed to annoy everyone else at their table.

- Someone will be unhappy that it ended so early; others will be unhappy that it ended too late for them to nip off to the nightclub.

And don't get me started on the Secret Santa gifts:

'I don't like what I received!'

'But I spent more on the gift I bought than the one I received!'

'Where's my gift? I haven't got one!'

'I don't want to be part of this.'

'I think we should all donate to charity instead.'

'I haven't brought my gift in on time to go into the pot with the others.' (This results in you having to go out of your way on the day before the gift-giving to buy three emergency gifts to cover for those that haven't yet arrived, just so everyone will receive something and the 'spirit of giving' remains untarnished – whilst you sit there gnashing your teeth and feeling very un-Christmassy.)

Here are some brave tips to help these activities run smoothly (and save your sanity!):

- Don't try to please absolutely everyone – it just isn't possible.

- If you are booking the party venue, make sure that you know what the budget is per person. If staff are paying to attend, check with a few colleagues as to whether the budget you are aiming at is manageable for them.

- Whatever you're planning, ask a small number of colleagues for their opinions to give you some guidelines for your decision-making. If they have been at the school or college for longer than you, ask them what has been done in the past at Christmas, what went well, what could have been better and if they have any advice for you in organising this year's arrangements.

- You might want to consider doing a survey of the staff to find out what the majority view is – do they want a meal, a dinner and dance, a pub evening, a quiz, a casino night? Obviously, you will inevitably end up with several groups who want different things, but hopefully you can settle on an option that works for the majority.

- Don't forget the importance of making sure that everyone can get home from the party – a lovely hotel out in the country might be a very nice venue, but not when you have a crowd of people all waiting for the one and only local taxi driver to get them home. If possible, plump for a city centre venue or at least one with good public transport links.

- For Secret Santa, there is quite often a rush at the end to buy last-minute gifts because someone has dropped out or hasn't brought their gift in. Rather than wait for this to happen, obtain some petty cash and purchase a couple of spare gifts in advance. Keep them safely stored in a drawer or cupboard in your office. If they are fairly generic items, you can always keep them in the office to give as gifts in the new year if they aren't needed.

- Don't let other people's disorganisation ruin your day. There are bound to be differences of opinion amongst the staff as to what constitutes a great party, and there is almost certainly going to be someone who complains about their Secret Santa gift. Don't stress about this too much – instead, let them know that you sympathise, but reiterate (gently) that it is nigh on impossible to please everyone.

So, what's my main bravery tip to you in this chapter? Once you have organised either the Christmas party or the Secret Santa for a year or two, but then start to dread Christmas coming round again because you know for certain that you will want to murder someone three days before the end of term (and, funnily enough, it will always be one of the same three people who you want to murder each year because they will always be unreliable), delegate the task to someone else next year! If, however, you love doing it, then keep doing it – just remember to have a Merry Christmas!

Oh, and while we're talking about delegating, let's look at it in more detail in the next chapter.

BRAVERY IS ... DELEGATING
TASKS TO SOMEONE ELSE

As a PA working in education, almost without doubt you will be given far too many tasks to carry out and, short of successfully cloning yourself, you will at some point need to delegate some of your work to a colleague. This should be looked on as a great opportunity for them – it enables them to develop within their role by increasing their current skills and knowledge and take on new levels of responsibility and accountability.

Delegating can be really challenging for you too though. If you are used to getting things done quickly to deadline, under pressure and to a consistently high standard, it can be quite scary to let go and hand a task over to a colleague, knowing that you don't have full control over what happens to that piece of work. If your co-worker doesn't have the same level of skills this can make it even scarier, so it can sometimes be tempting to carry out the task yourself, particularly if you believe that you could complete it in a much shorter length of time than it would take you to train your colleague to do it.

However, letting go is what it's all about: training a colleague to carry out a task, then showing them you have faith in them, that you honour their abilities and that you trust them. The additional bonus should be that, once they have been trained to take on the task and complete it to a certain level of proficiency, then you will be freed up to work on other projects yourself. Time to call on your Bravery SAS – you need diplomacy when delegating, as well as great decision-making and negotiating skills.

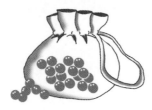

So, how can you delegate tasks effectively to allay fears on all sides?

- Priorities and best fit. Before you delegate a task to a colleague, think about getting the right fit. Decide on the priority: is it to get the work done quickly, or to help your co-worker to improve their skills? Look at the tasks that need to be delegated to others, and do your best to identify the right person to carry them out. For example, if Teri is great with PowerPoint and Philippa is skilled in using tables in Word, ask yourself whether you wish to allocate tasks to them based on their existing skills for the sake of speed and efficiency, or whether you want to assign them tasks that will challenge them and encourage them to broaden their skills. In some cases, it may be more appropriate to simply hand the presentation work to Teri and the tables to Philippa; in other cases, it might be really beneficial to do the opposite, to encourage Teri to improve her work in Word and Philippa to start using PowerPoint to a higher level.

- Expectations and details. Outline the scope of the tasks and make your expectations clear. If possible, provide a written explanation of what the task entails, and set reasonable deadlines in order to keep things on track.

- Did you get that? Make sure your colleagues know that they can come to you with questions if they need to. You may think you have given them a clear outline of what is required, but once you have left them to get on with it they might have further questions. If the task or project is complex, or needs them to learn new skills, check in early on to see how they are getting on and to ensure they are on-task. Is there anything preventing them from completing the task?

- Training needs. When delegating a task, make sure that your colleague knows how to actually carry out the work, and give them training if required. Yes, it may take you half an hour to talk them through something that would only take you 20 minutes to do, but if you train them properly they can perform the task from now on, saving you that 20 minutes every time.

- Encourage responsibility and decision-making. If at all possible, let your co-worker make the decision on how they will carry out the task – give them the responsibility for doing the work and let them choose their method of working. This may not apply for certain tasks which require following a rigidly prescribed method, but for less regimented tasks let them choose.

- Evaluate afterwards. How did they do? Evaluate the resulting work – the quality of the work done, the time it took and the finished product. If you and your colleague are both happy with these, then you don't need to review their methods of working. If, however, there were problems in any of these areas, then discuss how they carried out the work to see if you can offer any pointers for improvement.

- Acknowledgement and thanks. An absolutely essential part of successfully delegating any piece of work is to ensure that you give credit and praise to the person who has carried out the work. If your manager isn't already aware that you delegated the task, ensure that due credit is given to the right person at the right time and in an appropriate way. This will go a long way towards encouraging your colleagues to be receptive to other tasks being delegated to them in the future.

BRAVERY IS ... BEING A 'GATEKEEPER' FOR YOUR BOSS AND SPOTTING A COLD-CALLER AT 20 PACES

Another major element of the role of PA is to protect your head teacher or principal from others and to protect their time. This includes putting through the phone calls they need to take (and stopping those they don't) and welcoming legitimate visitors to their office at appropriate times (whilst fielding off all other requests for meetings which ought to be dealt with by somebody else in the school or college).

Key to your success in these areas will be to have a firm grip on who your boss knows, who they want to see and who they don't want to hear from, and being able to fend off everyone else in a polite manner – whilst being firm when necessary in order to deal with unwanted or persistent callers.

GET TO KNOW EVERYONE YOUR BOSS KNOWS

Everyone your boss knows is someone that you need to know too, so you need to obtain contact details for everyone they meet. Get to know your boss's contacts list inside out. If you are sure that the head doesn't know a caller personally, it's easier for you to field their phone call. This is invaluable when cold-callers and marketers call, asking for the head or principal on a first name basis and pretending they know them personally as a method of 'by-passing' the PA. A good PA is there to prevent

 Believe me, this happens – I have worked in two organisations where sales and recruiting staff were expressly trained in methods of 'getting past the gatekeeper', to push past the PA and to belittle the assistant into putting the call through to their manager. I thought this was a horrendous tactic – and PAs worldwide agree with me.

unwanted calls from getting through, so sales staff and recruiters would be far better positioned if they made friends with the PA during their calls instead of treating us badly and expecting us to put their calls through.

LAST CONVERSATIONS AND PERSONAL DETAILS

Keep notes on essential contacts in Outlook – what they do, where they are based, any personal information they share and a couple of facts about your last conversation. These are god-send bits of information for you (or your boss) to feed into your next conversations with them – it will show them that you were really listening and make them feel treasured and remembered. If you or the boss can bring into the conversation a question about something they mentioned on their last visit or call, you, your head or your school/college will stand out as caring and interested listeners.

LITTLE DETAILS COUNT FOR SUCH A LOT

Whenever your head or principal attends a conference or large meeting, ask them to gather business cards from the people they meet and talk with. Collate these in a shared contacts folder in Outlook that both you and your head can access.

If you have time, add photos to the folder for all the people for whom you have phone numbers. This should be easy for the members of staff at your own organisation as there is likely to be a folder on your computer network containing all their photos. (If there isn't, make one!) Adding photos means that, if your head/principal is using a smartphone linked to Outlook, the contact's photo will be displayed on the phone when they call, providing an instant visual reminder of who is calling. This is very useful if you have a large number of staff or your boss has lots of contacts around the world – seeing someone's face before answering their call can really help with memory recall.

I'm including here part of an article which I wrote on the subject of cold-callers: I think it is worth including as it contains the experiences and suggestions from a large number of PAs worldwide.

DEALING WITH COLD-CALLERS[1]

One classic timewaster in our role as PAs, and a vitally important person for us to 'weed out' from the calls that we put through to our head teacher or principal, is the cold-caller, the salesperson, the marketer – and what to do with them. I love cold-callers – I just couldn't eat a whole one.

Dealing with cold-callers comes up regularly during training courses and online PA networks – in particular, the type of cold-callers who think the best way to reach the principals/heads of our schools and colleges is to blast their way past the PA or receptionist with lies and counter-lies. PAs at my training courses have confirmed that this is an approach they have come across in both the corporate world and in education. Cold-callers can be the bane of our lives, as it is usually our role to be the gatekeeper between the outside world and our head/principal.

Over the years, I have heard from many salespeople trying to reach the head of my organisation by telephone in order to sell their products – many of these being services or items which have no relevance to our organisation, and many others who are pitching to completely the wrong person. Some callers will actually give details of their products, services or organisation while they are speaking to me, but a large number have attempted to use bullying or derogatory techniques to try to shame me into thinking that I am 'just a lowly PA' and that the best thing I could do would be to put them straight through to my manager, thank you very much. Others still have lied outright, saying that they met my boss at an event recently and he asked them to call him – which I always check so that I can report back to them when the boss says he's never heard of them. He retains all business cards from the people he meets, but he certainly doesn't have theirs.

We therefore need to be able to spot a cold-caller at 20 paces and have some techniques for how to deal with them.

The typical cold-caller is selling something, whether this is a product, a service or a person (many recruiters will try to sell you a new member of

---

1   Adapted with permission from: A Guide to Dealing with Cold Callers, *NAHPA* magazine, 31 (Autumn 2011), pp. 20–23.

staff who they believe is vital for your organisation). They will call and ask you to put them through to your manager – often without telling you who they are, where they are from or the nature of the call. Very few will admit that they are salespeople. When asked questions, they will be evasive or abrupt, sometimes even rude, in an attempt to get past you. Often they will imply that the call is personal or private, or highly confidential. As a confidential PA, though, they really ought to realise that *you* are the person they need to speak with!

Some cold-callers use ridiculously stupid tactics – I once took a call from someone who claimed to be my chief executive's GP, but I already knew the details of his GP's surgery, and my phone's screen showed that the caller's telephone number was from elsewhere in the country. Some callers have blatantly lied in an attempt to reach the boss, often mistakenly believing that he is the one-and-only decision-maker with whom they need to speak, while others will claim to be personal friends.

One key to handling cold-callers is to know your manager very well. Get to know what type of work he deals with, whom he deals with and the names of people he knows on a personal basis, as well as his business contacts. Take responsibility for storing and cataloguing the business cards that he receives – remind him to collect them when on his travels and to give them to you. When he does, ask for details from him on each person so that you can note these down. After all, if you know who he met recently and would be interested in hearing from, you are well prepared for when they call – and equally, you know who to turn away when they claim to be a personal or private contact.

When receiving a call from a number I don't recognise, I often pause for a second to click the Internet Explorer icon on my computer screen before answering the phone. In the first few seconds of the call I can type the phone number into Google to see if any useful information comes up, including whether they are listed on the internet as a nuisance caller.

Another tip is to get your manager's approval that all his calls have to go through you – and, in particular, all of his outside calls. This means no one in the organisation should be able to put a call through to him directly – they must put it through you first. In this way, you can immediately connect your boss with the important people – governors, board members, staff, genuine contacts, etc. – and hold off the others, saying that you need to know the caller's reason for calling before your manager will take the call.

When putting calls through, give your manager a quick précis of what you have been told by the caller, and remind him on a regular basis to let you know afterwards if a caller didn't speak to them on that topic. This not only helps you to stay on top of the various projects which your manager is working on, but it also informs you when a cold-caller has got through the net, so you know not to put that person through again.

I often think that if the salespeople could only do their market research better, then they would save us a huge amount of time – and themselves too! If they could aim their calls towards the most appropriate person at an organisation, rather than just trying to bulldoze their way to the manager/ principal/head teacher/chief executive/chairman, it would make everything so much easier.

I've received so many calls about recruitment which should have been directed to the HR manager rather than my boss, so many calls about corporate transport which should have been directed to the person who actually books corporate transport, but the salespeople concerned have been taught aggressive sales tactics that convince them that the only person at an organisation who can make a decision about anything is the head of that organisation.

In fact, most discussions about suppliers or service providers are held at other management levels, by the people responsible for using those services. In the vast majority of cases, it is only when proposals have been factored, costed, compared with existing providers and weighed up fully that the department manager will take the proposal to the head of the organisation for board approval.

From my various PA contacts, I've heard some absolute horror stories of cold-callers and salespeople who have stalked bosses or their assistants, pushed their way past receptionists, blagged their way into the building and made their way to the boss's office, or out-and-out lied on the phone in order to reach the head of the organisation – all in the name of making an unsolicited cold call. One salesperson apparently turned up at an organisation and hung around reception at the end of the day, then ambushed the chief executive as he was leaving the building. The chief executive curtly told the salesman, 'You either deal with my PA or no one – do not attempt to deal with me again.'

PAs around the world have shared their advice on dealing with cold-callers who insist they can speak with no one but the boss:

- 'I've told cold-callers: "All of the CEO's calls are taken by me. If you won't talk to me about it, I'm afraid I cannot put you through to him. If you will let me know what you are calling about, it may be more appropriate that your call goes to another member of staff who has responsibility for that area, and I'll try to put you through to them." This generally works, and I can then redirect their call as appropriate.'

- 'If a salesperson is upfront and honest, I will help direct them to the correct person. The latest pitch I've been getting is that my manager indicated an interest in their product online and asked that they get in touch with her, which I know is a total lie, and they call back every two or three weeks thinking that I'm not intelligent enough to recognise them and their lame pitch. If my manager was interested in an online product, then I'd be the one contacting them about it.'

- 'I ask the caller politely to recognise that part of my job is to screen the boss's calls and that I will not be able to put them through until I know what the call is about and can vet their call.'

- 'I've been on both sides of the desk – buyer and seller. As a buyer, I have the experience and knowledge to notice when a product has potential to help my company, and will be happy to talk to a sales rep. As a seller, I preferred to first invest the time and research to learn what problems my product could solve in an organisation, and then to focus on earning the right to both talk to and learn from the person who will benefit from the solution.'

- 'I think a lot of salespeople underestimate how much we actually know about the business our CEO is handling and what we need at that time. You are better off working directly with the PA – but keep in mind that a sales call (to us) is still a sales call. If we have a need, you have treated us with respect for our time and you aren't pushy, we will probably come to you first when we have a need.'

- 'Bottom of my list are sales calls from someone trying to use the CEO's first name. "Is Fred there?" Really! If they knew Fred so well, they'd have his mobile phone number or his direct line. Those calls just make me laugh. They can keep calling me – Fred will still be in a never-ending meeting.'

My own standard response to anyone cold-calling within my last role was that all of our strategic leadership group, including the principal, were very pressed for time and didn't make decisions on any product or service on the strength of a phone call. If the caller would please send an email with all the necessary details regarding their company, their product or service, their website and their contact details, then I would pass it on to the most relevant person in the academy. If that person then wanted to take things further, they would contact the caller. I asked the callers not to chase, but to accept that a nil response from us after a fortnight would mean that we did not require their services.

Some callers crop up on a regular basis, ringing year in, year out. This applies across all industries, including education. On the UK Academies PA network, which I chaired for five years, members regularly reported to each other when a known cold-caller started 'doing the rounds' again

– every year we received calls from the 'Government Initiatives Office' (which is nothing to do with the government), 'St James House' (nothing to do with royalty) and the 'Parliamentary Yearbook' (surprise, surprise – nothing to do with parliament), all of whom wished to urgently speak with our principals or head teachers on a personal, private matter. The actual purpose of each of their calls was to gain the head's ear about paying for marketing or editorial space in their publication. Given that we were all state-funded schools with very small marketing budgets (if any), most of our heads didn't want to be bothered with this sort of call and didn't wish to advertise in the publications, so we PAs worked to stop the calls from getting through. Year on year, PAs reported to the network that callers from these organisations were even using the same script which they attempted to read out over the phone. Year on year, we all turned them away and notified each other via the network, so that other academies could be forewarned about their imminent calls.

One of my PA connections contacted me a few years ago saying, 'I just had a caller who wants to speak to my MD about "Her Majesty's 85th birthday celebration". I asked if this call was an invitation to an event (knowing that it was not). "No, no!" said the caller. He could not speak with me – he *must* speak with my managing director personally. The caller was aggressive, supercilious and rude. I have had dealings with this "organisation" before. They must think we are morons. I have tipped off all our directors. If he calls back, I shall be having a bit of fun!'

Another PA who made regular visits to Buckingham Palace received the exact same call and asked her cold-caller which office they were in, as she might be able to pop in to see them that afternoon to discuss whatever they were calling about, before she made her way to the palace for a meeting. Needless to say, the caller became somewhat flustered and was unable to respond, then hung up the phone.

The final word on dealing with cold-callers has to go to the PA who related: 'I love cold calls: I recently told a double-glazing salesman that he should pop round to price up for me. I live on the eighth floor of a tower block.'

BRAVERY IS ... ALLOWING YOURSELF TO BE INSPIRED – AND ACTING ON IT

I'm all for inspiration. If something I do or say can inspire someone in some way, shape or form, I want to do it. Or if I see or hear someone else doing something amazing, I love the inspiration that this can give me. I'm a real believer in pointing a way forward for someone, or letting someone else sow a seed of inspiration in my head.

Who has inspired you during your life and your career? Who has shown confidence in you and your skills? Who have you looked up to and thought, 'I'd like to be like that'? Are there any teachers from your own education, people you have worked with, celebrities or historical figures who have resonated with you in some way?

Let's look at three interesting and useful exercises aimed to help with your thinking on inspiration.

1. WHO DO YOU FIND INSPIRATIONAL?

Take time to stop and think about the people who have inspired you. At first guess, your answer to, 'How many people have inspired you?' might be three or four. But if you take time to reflect on your life, there are probably far more than that. They might be members of your family, teachers, neighbours, people you have worked with at any point in your career, people you have met, people you have read about. They could be writers, sportspeople, TV personalities, historical figures, royalty, politicians, scientists, astronauts … anyone.

Whoever you find inspiring, consider what they are doing that you admire and try to work out how they are able to keep on doing what they do. Then try to use that for yourself in your own challenges. Use this person as a virtual mentor – when you face a difficulty, imagine one of your inspirationalists at their most successful and ask yourself, 'How would *they* handle this issue?'

My list of individuals who have inspired me includes colleagues who I've looked up to, friends who have suffered terrible illnesses bravely and people who have achieved something amazing when faced with incredible odds.

In the Resources section at the back of the book I've listed several books by PA trainers – people who have written about their experiences as PAs – plus there are several PA-related websites where you can learn from other PAs. Any of these could become one of your inspirationalists for the future.

2. HOW HAVE YOU BEEN INSPIRED BY THE PEOPLE IN YOUR LIFE?

Write your name in the middle circle below. In the other circles, write down the names of anyone who has had a direct positive influence on you in your life and/or career: people who have inspired you, had confidence in you or pushed you to do your best. While doing this, think about who they are, your relationship with them at the time, what happened, how you felt then and how you feel about the experience now.

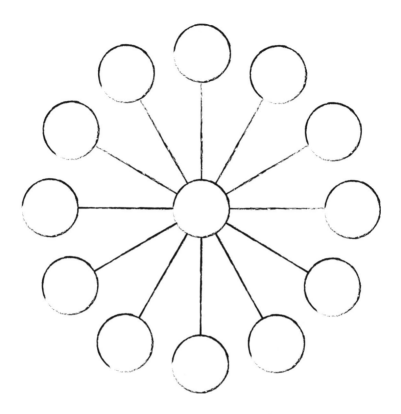

Your influencers/inspirationalists

For my own part, two of my key inspirationalists were a deputy head teacher who predicted (when I was 12 years old) that I would attend university, and my English teacher (when I was 14) who suggested that I could go into teaching as she felt I was good at helping others in the class. The seeds of inspiration were sown. These two women inspired me to train to be a teacher. They showed confidence in my skills and ability which, in turn, gave me the confidence to feel that I could do what they suggested. From the age of 12 onwards, I knew I would go to university – because I'd already been told that I would.

3. HOW HAVE YOU INSPIRED SOMEBODY ELSE BY YOUR ACTIONS?

Once you have reflected on the people who have influenced you, I'd like to ask you to complete the exercise again, but thinking about your life from another angle: consider whether there are any people who, if they were asked to complete this same exercise, would name *you* as one of their influencers. Who have you had a positive impact on, and in what way?

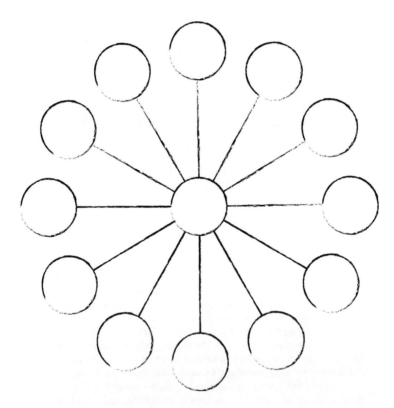

Who have you inspired?

Recognising that we have been inspired by someone else's actions can be really helpful in understanding the paths that we have chosen to take in our lives.

Leading on from this, realising that we can have a similarly inspiring effect on others, can be an equally worthwhile experience, demonstrating to us our worth in society. All too often, we work hard, work harder, work harder still – in our lives and in our jobs – without receiving recognition for what we do. It's good, therefore, to be able to remind ourselves every now again of our worth.

 On my own first attempt at working through these three simple exercises, I felt quite emotional when thinking about certain people and their positive influences in my life. I relayed this to a friend, who told me that she found me inspiring in several ways – which I had not previously recognised in our relationship – and it felt quite humbling to hear of my positive impact on her life.

BRAVERY IS ... SPOTTING
BAD BEHAVIOUR AND DOING SOMETHING ABOUT IT

Whether you work in an office where everyone gets along well or you have the usual office communication mishaps, how you communicate – both verbal and written – with others should always be professional.

Here are some brave behaviour tips for maintaining a healthy atmosphere in your office:

- Respect territory, whether it's someone's office space (e.g. desk, office), projects, relationships, personal space, etc.

- Be prompt for meetings. It indicates that you care and shows respect to the person who called the meeting.

- Contribute positively to discussions. Be a part of the solution, not the problem.

- If you don't know something, don't pretend you do. It is acceptable to say, 'I'm not sure about that, but I will find someone who is an expert and report back.'

- Return calls by the next business day. Many schools offer a 24-hour promise to contact parents – if you don't, why not consider this for your school? You know how frustrated you get when someone doesn't return your call!

- Be respectful of other people's time. Don't send them joke emails or useless printed material just because you can.

- Keep in mind that we can all have a bad day. When a colleague is experiencing a genuine personal crisis, think of this person before yourself and offer to help.

- Always return borrowed items promptly. (No, just because you've had someone's stapler for three days, and you like it, doesn't mean you can keep it!)

- Never repeat something that could be detrimental to a person's reputation. In other words, if what you say could harm a person's reputation or make them lose a position of high esteem or honour, don't say it.

- Learn to point out a mistake without 'blaming and shaming'. For example, if Sarah forgot to call a vendor about a delivery, don't highlight the fact. Sarah knows she forgot to make the call, you know she forgot and so might other people. Simply say, 'Can we work that call back into your already busy schedule?' The goal is to get the call made and the information obtained.

If a member of staff is uncooperative, bad tempered in the workplace or rude to colleagues or students, it can damage your school's or college's reputation and harm morale for all.

And when you excuse them, thinking, 'But it's only one person being awkward,' it is worth remembering that it only takes one difficult person to poison the atmosphere for everyone. This means it is vital to deal with unacceptable behaviour as soon as it arises. If we are all about showing our pupils and students how to be good upstanding citizens for the future, we have to carry these attributes forward ourselves as adults: allowing bad behaviour by colleagues to continue unchecked can send out the signal that it is tolerated and even acceptable.

If you notice the pattern of a staff member speaking inappropriately to students, governors, directors or sponsors, or objecting to reasonable requests, deal with it quickly so that it doesn't become a habit. For major issues, of course, the principal/head teacher or the staff member's department head needs to be informed and it may be more appropriate for them to take responsibility for dealing with it, but for misdemeanours that you come across in your working day, it should be your responsibility to do something about it.

BRAVE TIPS WHEN SPEAKING TO COLLEAGUES ABOUT BAD BEHAVIOUR

Time for you to dig into your bravery bag – using courage, calmness, dignity, negotiating skills and determination.

- Don't back out of bringing up difficult issues.
- Allow a little time for things to cool off.
- If you must confront a colleague, pick an appropriate time and place. Barging in when they are in a classroom, meeting or up against a tight deadline is unfair and unprofessional.
- Deal with problems privately, away from the listening ears and prying eyes of other colleagues or students.
- You might begin by asking them how they are feeling about work and whether they have any problems. Difficult behaviour is often an expression of an underlying problem that is not being addressed.
- If they reveal a work-related issue, try to help or find helpful resources for them.
- If they reveal a personal difficulty, you could remind them that your role is to be a confidential PA. Offer support in the form of a listening ear and, if you can, provide some practical help.
- Explain that you are asking them these questions because you are concerned about something in their behaviour which is having a negative effect. If your school or college has a written behaviour policy or code of conduct to refer to, this should make your task easier.

- Be prepared with specific examples of their behaviour and be ready to explain the negative impact it could have on the school/college/university.

- Come armed with practical suggestions on how to avoid this problem in the future. Explain your concerns in a calm, reasoned tone and be willing to listen to the other person's side of the story – perhaps there are factors of which you are unaware.

This may well be all that is needed. Your colleague might not have been fully aware of what they were doing, or just bringing it up with them may embarrass them (or encourage them) into changing their attitude. They may also be grateful for the chance to get something off their chest; be prepared to acknowledge their feelings, but make sure you get your own message across.

If, however, your informal intervention fails, it may well be that you have to pass the matter on to a more senior member of staff to ask them to take it further. Don't be afraid to do this – it's not 'snitching' on a colleague if you are putting forward a valid complaint about something which is having a negative impact on the college.

BRAVERY IS ... DEMONSTRATING TO STUDENTS THAT BEING A PA IS A GREAT CAREER CHOICE

We've already looked at the people who have inspired you in your life – and those you may have inspired by your own actions. How can you develop this further, in terms of inspiring some of the pupils at your school, or students at your college or university, to become the personal assistants and administrators of the future?

As the use of technology continues to grow, our pupils and students are more and more familiar with typing documents, using spreadsheets, creating PowerPoint presentations and reports within their studies – all of which are vital skills that could stand them in great stead in a PA role, if they would just consider it as a career path.

In the past, secretarial work was often regarded as a 'fall back' job – in that women and teenage girls were encouraged to learn to type in case they needed a job at some point, often in relatively lowly position. But things have changed, and the role of PA has developed enormously since the early secretarial days.

For many people, becoming a PA or administrator wasn't necessarily an active career choice but something which they drifted into over time. In early 2014, I conducted a survey on LinkedIn in one of the discussion groups that I run for PAs. Over 2,000 UK-based PAs in all industries, including education, responded. One of the questions was: 'How many of us in childhood said, "I want to be a secretary/PA/EA/admin when I grow up"? Did you choose this as a career, did you drift into it or are you on your way somewhere else entirely?'

DID YOU CHOOSE TO BE A SECRETARY/PA/EA/ADMIN?

I had no idea what I wanted to be — 14%

I definitely didn't want to be an admin — 12%

I had different dreams and drifted into it — 44%

I saw admin as just a stepping stone — 11%

I wanted to be an administrator — 18%

0% 10% 20% 30% 40% 50%

Source: Survey on 'PAs, EAs, Vas and Senior Admins' group, LinkedIn (March 2014)

Only around 1 in 7 of the respondents reported that they had actively wanted to become a PA, with a further 1 in 9 seeing the role as a stepping stone to something else. These figures might be low because, in our childhood, the vast majority of us had no idea what a personal assistant was, or because the only vision we had of an administrative role was of the old-fashioned stereotype of the 1950s secretary being bullied by their boss.

How do we change these figures? By inspiring others to join the profession! It has been estimated that around a quarter of the world's working population work in an administrative role of some sort, but as we've seen from the clichéd secretary character who is continually trotted out in films and TV shows, there is still a common misconception about the role of the PA/EA/secretary (see page 61 for more on this).

An Australian National PA survey in 2013 asked PAs about the differences in the PA role from that of secretary, and reported the following as the main results:

- Responsibilities (20.1%)
- How the role is perceived by others (17.7%)
- Skills (17.3%)
- Career path (11.7%)
- Qualifications and education levels (11.3%)[1]

If the mainstream media doesn't show that the role of PA has moved on so much from the 1950s secretary then we need to be the ones doing it. Do you like or love your role as a PA? If you do – then tell someone! Talk to your children or your friends' children about their career choices, and ask them if they have considered a role in administration as a PA. Do the same with the pupils at your school or college.

Do you eat your lunch in your office or at tables with other staff? If you do, stop doing this and instead go and sit with a group of pupils and talk with them about their day, their lives, their aspirations. Build a relationship with them over the next few weeks. Ask them what they want to do for a career, tell them what you do, describe how you feel about your job. Find some common ground that you can talk to them about (see page 157 on watching television) and then share some of your experiences with them.

---

1   Statistics cited in Leo D'Angelo Fisher, Getting Serious: The Personal Assistant Role Is Changing for the Better, Despite Some Unusual Requests, *BRW* (8 November 2013). Available at: http://www.brw.com.au/p/leadership/ getting_serious_despite_personal_LClRdv19F8BB4KjBf2WbeM/.

Does your school or college teach any form of business studies? If it does, talk with the course leader and see if you can become involved in any way – perhaps by demonstrating a skill to a group of pupils or by talking with them about the various administrative roles they might move into with a good qualification in business studies.

Does your school or college involve students in running the reception desk? Many schools, in particular, are now doing this – giving pupils in the school the opportunity to spend a day on reception to experience being a 'first point of contact' and an ambassador for the school. If your school or college does this, get involved in making sure that the pupils have an active, useful and interesting set of tasks to do during their day, to give them a positive view of working in an administrative role.

There are many other ways in which you could give someone else the idea of becoming a PA as a great career choice. For example, if you at some point write an article and it is published in a PA-related magazine, stick a copy of the article on your office door and tell people about it. If you give an hour of your time per week to work with an after-school club – whether or not it has anything to do with the role of PA – you will build relationships with the pupils who attend, so talk with them. Let them see how much you enjoy your career, how challenging you find it and how satisfying it can be. None of us will ever be inspired by someone who sounds bored or fed up with their job, so when you are talking about what you do make sure they see your passion and enjoyment.

Talk to them about the various skills and qualifications they would need to become a PA. It can be a really proud moment to sit with a group of pupils discussing how they could become junior PAs, and to hear them then talk enthusiastically about what they could do with their futures. Then, once you have inspired one or more pupils, start the same conversation with another group.

BRAVERY IS ... CONTROLLING
THE ENORMOUS NUMBER OF DEMANDS ON YOUR TIME

Do any of the items in this list of some of the major interruptions to the days of many PAs look familiar to you?

- Telephone calls (both making and receiving).
- People dropping into your office.
- Lost documents or files – and wasting time looking for them because they have been misfiled.
- Someone else's emergency (due to bad planning on their part).
- Being disorganised – flitting from one thing to another and never finishing anything.
- Constantly changing the priorities of the various tasks in your in-tray.
- Computer problems – the 'blue screen of death'.
- Having to repeat requests to people as they didn't listen or read your email correctly the first time – or because your original message was ambiguous.
- Running late (you and others) – arriving late for work or joining a meeting after it has started.

- Doing other people's work for them because the work has been given to you and you haven't delegated it.
- Badly organised or badly chaired meetings.
- Fixing something that was done poorly first time round.
- Indecisive colleagues – or your own indecision about how to do things.
- Distractions in your office – other people making calls, your office being a thoroughfare for everyone to walk through, constant noise.
- Being micro-managed to the nth degree.
- Having to fill in lots of forms (in triplicate) because procedures are too bureaucratic.

Some of these are things that *you* can change. Some are things that require *other people* to change things. Others are things that would require *organisation-wide* changes in policies.

Let's concentrate for the time being on the things that are within your control. A good course or book on time management will help you with most of these, but here are some suggestions for the most common problems you will face.

PLANNING YOUR DAY/WEEK

Being better organised can help you to cope with the multiple demands on your time every day. How can you do this? By planning your day and/or week. Obviously, there will be some things you cannot plan for – that is the nature of being a PA/administrator in education. There will always be things that crop up urgently which require your attention, but for the things that you know you need to work on, you can plan.

Some good tips for planning your week well include:

- Keep an up-to-date list of everything that you currently have to do (your action list).

- Find 30 minutes at the same time every week to plan your week – identifying priorities.

- Use your diary to book time to complete major activities and also for some of your more mundane administrative tasks (e.g. reviewing inbox, filing, managing emails or meeting preparation, planning).

- Check your diary and your action list every morning to establish your priorities for the day. Write them on one page of your notepad and keep it on your desk. If you do nothing else today, do these and you will have had a good day!

- Review. As priorities change, be prepared to adapt and be flexible.

MANAGING YOUR TIME

- When planning, add a time limit to how long you will work on each task. The 'Pomodoro technique' (named after the Italian kitchen timer in the shape of a tomato or *pomodoro*) advocates spending 25 minutes on each task (with a possible 5 minute overrun) so you can concentrate on two tasks per hour.

- Know your deadlines for each piece of work. If you've got an open-ended task it is all too easy to leave it, and then be in a panic when suddenly you are asked when it will be ready.

- Learn how to say no (see page 125).

- Have a clock in plain view of your desk.

- Set reminders on your computer for 15 minutes before a meeting to give yourself adequate time to finish up before you have to head off.

- Find ways to block out distractions (e.g. you could use an MP3 player or noise-cancelling headphones to block out noise if you are in a busy workplace).

- Don't sweat the small stuff. Don't fuss about unimportant details.

- Prioritise your work. If it's very important, and very urgent, do it first.

- Delegate work where possible. Even if you have to spend time now in training a colleague to do the task, this at least means you can just give them more of the same work at a later date and they should be able to get on with it.

- With colleagues who come to you asking you to do something for them because they don't know how say, 'I will show you now – watch me – and then next time you will be able to do it for yourself.'

- End phone calls when you need to.

- Schedule in some 'grey time'. Don't give yourself back-to-back tasks all day in your planner, as you will need some time as a buffer for all the emergencies that are sure to come in.

HANDLING INTERRUPTIONS

If you can, develop some methods for dealing with interruptions. Research in 2012 by Professor Gloria Mark of the University of California has shown that the average interruption in a workplace can take up to 23 minutes from start of the interruption to returning to the original task, and that the majority of interruptions are actually of fairly low priority or urgency.[1] So, if you experience just a small number of interruptions per day, you can easily lose an hour or more of time which could have been spent on major tasks, but is instead used in dealing with lower level tasks which are brought to you throughout the day by others. Sometimes an interruption may only be quite short but can have time-consuming ramifications (e.g. how often do you attempt to phone somebody but they are not available, so you spend more time later in the day trying to reach them? – so an interruption of being asked to make a few simple phone calls can end up taking up several segments of your day to

---

1   Gloria Mark, Stephen Voida and Armand Cardello, 'A Pace Not Dictated By Electrons': An Empirical Study of Work Without Email (2012). Available at: http://www.ics.uci.edu/~gmark/Home_page/Research_files/CHI%202012.pdf.

carry out). If an interruption comes when you are in the middle of a really complicated piece of work, it is more difficult to pick up your train of thought after the interruption, so the effect is even more significant. If you have planned properly (using your diary) then it is far easier to avoid interruptions. You will be more aware of the time you have to complete a task, and how well you are progressing.

Interruptions can take many forms, so here are some common problems and some brave methods to resolve them:

- The arrival of new email:
  - > Turn off notifications on your email package so you are not tempted to read every new message as and when it arrives.
- Receiving a phone call:
  - > If you are frantically busy in the middle of a particular task, ask the caller if you can call them back in 20 minutes when you will be able to give them your full attention.
  - > Ask a colleague to cover your phone for an hour a day to allow you some space for concentrating on particular project work, and do the same for your colleague to help them out.
- Making a phone call:
  - > Set aside 20 minutes to make four or five calls one after the other, and try to get through all of them in that time.
  - > Standing up while you make calls may seem a little bizarre but it prompts you to keep calls short.
  - > Start each call by announcing the purpose of the call, and try to keep the call to that point.
- Someone popping into your office:
  - > Stand up with a notepad in your hand and walk towards the door as if you are going out.
  - > Let them know that you only have two or three minutes as soon as they arrive.
  - > Don't let them sit down! Take a note of what they need, then usher them out of the door with a promise to get back to them at an appropriate time.

> Say, 'I am very busy at the moment. How about if you pop back at 2 p.m. or phone me then about whatever you need?'

> Develop an 'open door = available, closed door = busy' policy for your office.

 I learned a great method for avoiding interruptions when I was working in an enormous open-plan space. All of the admin assistants and PAs had a folded red card on their desk: if the card was flat on the desk, or not in sight, this indicated that they were free for anyone to approach them with questions or queries; but if the card was propped up on the desk it meant, 'I'm busy on a task, please come back later.' Of course, this is not going to work in emergencies or with your direct boss – and it certainly won't work if you have the red card standing up on your desk all day, every day, or if all of your admin team have their red cards up at the same time. But if a system along these lines can help you to avoid a small number of interruptions at a particularly busy time, then great!

And for any methods that you use or develop and which work for you – *share them with others*!

BRAVERY IS ... STRESSING
THE IMPORTANCE OF NOT GETTING STRESSED OUT

Is the pressure of your role getting to you? Time (or, more pertinently, not having enough of it) is often named as the number one concern for most people in the workplace. There is never enough time to accomplish everything, let alone managing all of the various priorities that PAs have to deal with.

If in your role you have a continual, unrelenting stream of tasks, it can feel very daunting, as there seems to be no light at the end of the tunnel. So here are some of my brave tips to help maximise your effectiveness and make time work for you.

- Put it in writing. The simple act of putting words on a page (either on paper or your computer screen) allows you to see exactly what it is you have to do and to prioritise the tasks.

- Create your own due dates. You know whether or not you are a good manager of your own time. However, since most of us are not, include realistic due dates with each listed task based on your work habits. For example, if you know that project X is due next Monday, and it will take you three days to complete, set a cushioned due date of five days. This will ensure that you start early enough and allow for any unforeseen circumstances.

- Spend a few minutes on a task that you really enjoy. If you have a really difficult piece of work to complete and you feel stuck or like you are drowning in it, consider stopping that task for 15 minutes and doing something else. Spend five minutes making yourself a fresh cup of tea or coffee or going for a quick walk, then spend the remaining 10 minutes on a more pleasant or quick-and-easy task. This can help to change your mood, making it easier to continue with the difficult task when you return to it. Quite often, taking a break and thinking about something different for a few minutes can give your brain time to review what you were doing and hopefully you can return to it reinvigorated.

- Do something for you! Commit to including one task on your to-do list that is just for you. Maybe your work area could use a little sprucing up, so straight after lunch do a 10 minute tidy round. Or get up out of your chair during the mid-afternoon slump and take the walk you keep saying you should be taking. It might even be scheduling a small personal task – take that bonus or raise and spend it on yourself in a quick shopping trip at lunchtime or via the internet.

- Don't procrastinate. We always put off the toughest task until last, when, in fact, we should be doing just the opposite. Completing that tough task first provides a tremendous relief and can actually motivate us to a higher level, so that we work more efficiently and effectively on those tasks that aren't so hard.

- Plan a personal treat for your spare time. Make plans for some special personal time this weekend – it might be a massage, a day at the spa, a haircut, a good movie, a special meal or a night out with friends. Knowing you have a treat planned at the weekend can help you through the next few days, particularly if it's a stressful time at work.

- Minimise time-wasting activities. Make shorter phone calls. Thank visitors to your office for their time, and then see them out of the door swiftly and smoothly – don't let them linger. If you need to stand over the photocopier for any length of time to copy some highly confidential documents, take your office mobile phone with you and make a few calls whilst you are waiting for the copying to finish or make some notes on how to tackle your next tasks.

● Just say no. There are only so many hours in a day, and if it cannot be done, it cannot be done. Even Superwoman/Superman/Super-PA can't do everything *all* of the time. (See page 125 for help on saying no.)

BRAVERY IS ... CREATING YOUR PURPLE FOLDER[1]

Every PA should have a purple folder – the one and only purple folder (a standout colour and easily spottable) in your office. The purple folder is the bible to your job.

Quite often, one of our biggest worries as PAs in busy schools and colleges is that we are indispensable – that our head teacher or principal simply cannot manage without us. Most organisations cope very well when the boss is out at meetings or on leave, as their PA keeps things running smoothly in their absence. But when the PA goes off on sick leave, or takes another job, it can often seem like the whole world is coming to an end back in the office! Files can't be found, no one knows who to contact about what, the boss can't find his spare papers, the coffee machine goes on a blink – and that's all just in the first morning.

Whilst it's lovely to feel appreciated, and to know that the work we do is vitally important to the boss and to the organisation, this can lead to difficulties. For example, if you feel so needed by your boss that you cannot possibly go off on sick leave or take a holiday, or you delay having a family for a year or two because there will be no one there who is able to do your job as well as you, then you need to do something about it. And fast!

Take action before illness (or life) catches up with you by creating a purple folder – your job bible – and filling it with detailed instructions on how to perform various aspects of your role, including lists of things to be done at particular times of the school year, useful contacts, where you file things, passwords to particular websites or computer packages that you know and use on a day-to-day basis – in short, everything that's needed if you are not in the office for whatever reason.

---

1   This chapter is adapted with permission from: The purple folder: the PAs guidebook, *NAHPA* magazine, 34 (Autumn 2012), pp. 9–11.

This means that when you are taken ill, break a leg, go on maternity leave, take a well-earned holiday or even leave your role to move on to pastures new, the person who next sits down at your desk can pick up the purple folder, look through it and get on with covering your job or starting their new role.

Not only is the purple folder the perfect handover folder when changing jobs, but it's also the key to listing your achievements for your yearly performance appraisal as it catalogues all the major tasks that you do. It gives you great ammunition and evidence when the boss says, 'So what have you done this year that you are particularly proud of?'

The purple folder can also be used as a training guide for an internal talent pool of employees who will be ready to step into your role. And when you leave, it will be the perfect guide for your boss on working out the type of person and the skills needed by your successor.

WHY A PURPLE FOLDER?

There are two reasons why you should choose a purple folder:

1. Most offices are filled with single-colour folders and files, usually black or green. So, having one solitary stand-out folder on your shelf of a completely different colour makes it easy to find for your boss, a colleague or a temp in your absence. You can simply tell them, 'All the information you need is in my purple folder.' When there's only one purple folder amongst all of the many folders on the shelves in your office, your boss or colleague has a fighting chance of finding and selecting the right one!

2. Purple is my favourite colour!

HOW TO SET UP YOUR PURPLE FOLDER

1. The first simple starting point is to order a purple folder from your stationers. Buy a few packs of dividers too, so that it can be separated into sections. As you go on, you will see that this list of sections can get quite long, so I'd advise that the folder you buy is a lever arch one rather than a smaller D-ring binder.

2. Start creating sections and add a piece of paper for each one listing the things you think ought to go in that section. Some examples are:

   〉 Opening section describing the role, who you work for, details of the leadership team, members of the rest of the admin team (including who does what).

   〉 Copy of the school's yearly calendar.

   〉 Details on how to access your computer files (username, password, file locations, etc.).

   〉 Daily tasks (which can include sub-dividers for specific Monday, Tuesday, Wednesday, Thursday and Friday tasks if need be).

   〉 Weekly tasks.

   〉 Termly tasks, including things that need to be done before the next term or half-term starts (subdivided into terms).

   〉 Major contacts (including leadership team, admin team and governors).

   〉 Other useful contacts within the school (reprographics, IT support, heads of year groups/houses, behaviour support, school nurse, etc.).

   〉 Major outside contacts and suppliers (school sponsors, stationery suppliers, drinks machine suppliers, local taxi company, suppliers of your prospectus/student planners/ teacher planners, etc.).

   〉 PA contacts at other local schools and the head teachers/ principals they work for.

> List of regular meetings that the boss attends (both internally and externally) and the chairs of each group with contact details.

> Thank you messages and notes of praise.

3. Rather than trying to make a completely exhaustive list of sections at the very beginning of creating your purple folder, narrow your focus a little – stop and think about the last week or the last month. What regular tasks have you done? List them and then put the list into the appropriate weekly or monthly tasks section in the folder. This will become the contents page for this section.

4. Start writing up one or two tasks per day if you can. Try not to go into immense detail – just a write-up describing the task, what your approach was, how you carried it out and what further steps might be needed later should suffice. A good PA or admin assistant stepping into your shoes (whether temporarily or for a new role) should be able to work out how to do the things you describe, so don't spend forever going into minute detail. If you want to handwrite it, that's fine, but you will probably find it easier to type it as you can include screen-dumps (pictures of what you did and how) as useful reminders. Start each task on a new page.
Aim to write up between five and ten tasks in a week, perhaps setting aside 15 minutes a day for this. Some weeks you may only get a couple of tasks written up, but in other weeks you may get several more done as they are shorter to write up, so don't panic. As you finish cataloguing each task, print it out and add it to your folder – and write the title onto a contents sheet at the front of its section in the folder and in the front of the folder. This way, anyone going through the folder can search either by the contents list or how regularly a task comes along.

5. Keep steadily working through the daily, weekly and termly tasks that you do, covering all the regular ones and making a few notes on those odd tasks that crop up here or there. They might not happen again, but how you went about solving them could help someone to resolve another out-of-the-ordinary task when it comes along.

6. Review where you are up to and congratulate yourself every now and again – you are well on the way to having written your job bible! Look back at the sections you have done and check to see if there is anything that needs moving from one section to another – for example, something might occur more often than you thought, so you move it to the weekly section.

7. Some of the sections will be quicker to complete than others – for example, you will probably have all the details you need for your contacts section in Outlook, so it should take very little time to copy and paste them into a Word document. Furthermore, staff lists, organisation charts, internal telephone lists and so on should already be in existence, so they can just be printed out and inserted into the folder.

8. If you think of new sections or new items to add to other sections, just jot them down, one per page, and add the pages to the folder. Don't worry if you haven't got time to write them up yet – the pages will serve as a reminder of what you need to work on when you do have time.

So, your folder is in preparation and you are working on it week by week. Now what?

- Tell people about it. One major part of making your purple folder work for you is to tell two groups of people about it. The first group is your fellow PAs or admin staff at your school, so in the event that you are off they know to check in the folder to see what regular tasks they could be covering while you are away. The second group is your senior leadership team, including your boss, so that they know you are doing all you can to have contingency plans in place for when you are away or change jobs.

- Use it for reminders throughout the year of what you need to get done and when. If you have put items into your folder in daily/weekly/termly order, you can see at a glance what tasks you need to do at the same times year in, year out.

- Use it to inform your next appraisal or performance review. Go through the folder before your annual review or performance appraisal as a reminder of your numerous achievements throughout the year. Having a list of the major tasks that you have carried out readily available can prompt your memory – for many of us, our jobs in schools are so frenetic and so busy that it is difficult to think back to what happened during the year and be able to pick out instances of things we did particularly well.

● An additional section you may like to add to your purple folder would be a section for any thank you messages or notes of particular praise or accolades. These can be particularly useful in evidencing that the chair of governors was delighted with your organisational work on a major event, or that a parent found your help and guidance very useful – more ammunition for pushing for a raise, promotion, job title re-grading or recognition of higher responsibilities.

WHAT'S IN IT FOR YOU?

Preparing your purple folder – and maintaining it as a document continually in progress – is also of enormous benefit for you personally. For example:

● When preparing for your yearly performance appraisal.

● When rewriting your job description to suit your current tasks and responsibilities.

● When your job is being re-graded.

● When you want somewhere to keep track of your CPD.

● When you want somewhere to keep notes of thanks you have received.

● When you want to apply for a job elsewhere, as it can give you great prompts on your skills to list in your application.

WHAT'S IN IT FOR YOUR SCHOOL/COLLEGE?

Your purple folder is ideal for helping your boss and your colleagues:

● When you are off on sick leave or maternity leave.

● When you leave your job or retire, or when you are promoted to another position and a replacement is required, as it can aid in producing a realistic job description and person specification.

● When someone new starts in your role, as handover notes.

So what are you waiting for? Go and get a purple folder and start making some notes to put in it! Do remember – it should be considered as a 'work in progress' as your role will develop over time, so please don't leave it to go dusty on a shelf – use it on a regular basis and keep updating it.

BRAVERY IS ... KNOWING
WHEN TO SAY 'NO' TO THE BOSS

Most of the PAs that I've met have reported on their difficulty over saying no to more work. I think this is related to the very nature of the role of PA – to assist in whatever way we can. One of the main difficulties seems to be knowing *how* and *when* to say no – including the actual wording that could be used in different situations. So, here are some of my favourite responses that I've pulled together over the years – some from my own arsenal, others from the PAs that I've met and trained.

TO UNREASONABLE REQUESTS TO PUSH A JOB TO THE FOREFRONT OVER OTHER TASKS – BE CALM AND FIRM:

'That's not something I can do right now – the task I'm currently working on has to take priority.'

'It's not possible with the resources that I currently have. We could look at getting some help from another department – or perhaps even passing the task in its entirety to them – but there isn't time for me to get it done here right now.'

WHEN OVERLOADED – DON'T APOLOGISE FOR NOT BEING SUPERWOMAN/SUPERMAN/SUPER-PA:

'I'm tied up for the rest of the day on a higher priority project, so the earliest I could start on it would be first thing in the morning.'

'I have several other tasks that are equal priority, and it's not going to be possible to get them all completed at once. Could you let me know which is the ultimate highest priority item, so I can get that one done first, then I'll work through the others.'

WHEN THE REQUESTER SHOULD BE CAPABLE OF DOING IT FOR THEMSELVES:

'OK, I will show you this one time, so that next time you can do it for yourself. Here, sit down and do what I tell you to do ...'

WHEN IT'S NOT YOUR JOB – TRY TO POINT THE WORK IN THE RIGHT DIRECTION:

'I know that it's tempting to pass this to me to do, because I always show a bright smiley face and take on almost every task you give me, but realistically this particular task is the responsibility of X in the Y department, and that puts me in a difficult position with them when they find out that you give their work to me. Are you OK with me giving this to them, or would you like to take it to them yourself?'

WHEN THE BOSS SAYS THEY WANT YOU TO DO IT AS THEY TRUST YOU TO DO IT RIGHT:

'I know my role is to be your go-to person for almost everything, but you need to start trusting other staff in the same way that you trust me. There are so many talented people on the staff here. If you really think I'm the only person who would get this job done in the way you want it to be done, let me train them to do it that way – then they can do it the future. That will then leave me available to help you on other projects to a higher level.'

WHEN ASKED/TOLD TO DO SOMETHING OUTSIDE THE REALMS OF YOUR JOB DESCRIPTION:

Consider whether or not you want to do it. Some PAs might be more than happy to be carrying out personal work for their bosses (e.g. booking family holidays or dental appointments), whilst others may be very clear on remaining rigidly within the realms of business. It is dependent on the unique relationship between each PA and their boss, so there can be no hard and fast rule that all PAs should adhere to.

WHEN THE PERSON ISN'T ACTUALLY ONE OF YOUR MANAGERS – THEY ARE JUST SOMEONE WANTING TO THINK THEY ARE:

'I have a lot of high priority work to do for the principal/head teacher/deputy vice chancellor, so I'm not able to help you. How about you speak with the admin team and ask if someone has some time available?'

WHEN ASKED/TOLD TO DO SOMETHING BEYOND YOUR MORAL OR ETHICAL BOUNDARIES:

A trainer told me a few years ago of having heard from a PA that her boss's ex-wife had died suddenly. The couple had a grown-up daughter, and the manager asked his PA to break the news to her. She drew the line at doing this and refused. He then attempted to make an official complaint about her to the HR department for not doing what he asked. The HR director upheld the PA's decision to say no. The PA stayed loyal to this company after her manager left because they had believed in her right to say no and to maintain her personal/moral boundaries.

WHEN ASKED/TOLD TO DO SOMETHING WHICH YOU SUSPECT MAY BE ILLEGAL:

There are regular items in our newspapers of PAs being asked (or told) by their bosses to do something that is wrong – morally, legally or ethically. Regardless of whether or not the PA in question knew the importance of the tasks they were given, or whether they were aware of the task's significance in a legal sense, the reports give us food for thought.

If you were presented with a task that you thought might be wrong or illegal, where would you draw the line? Where do you set limits in your working relationships? Where do you draw the boundaries? When does a PA have the right to say no to their boss? I'm sure all of us will have very different perspectives on this.

Throughout all of the above issues, it is important that these boundaries are considered and discussed – clarity of expectations of how a PA and boss are working together. Our own personal internal value systems are what drives where we draw our boundaries – what behaviour we expect and what we will accept from others – and these are different for each one of us.

Here are some questions to help you reflect on your business ethics and boundaries:

- When was the last time that you spent time considering your own value system/moral compass/where you draw your ethical lines?

- If your boss asked you to do something outside of your own value system, how would you navigate that without damaging the working partnership?

- Where does your role start and, just as importantly, where does your role stop?

BRAVERY IS ... CHALLENGING HABITUAL COMPLAINERS AND ASKING THEM FOR THEIR SOLUTIONS TO THE ISSUE

Have you ever had a conversation with somebody who whines and complains about something, but seems to do nothing about it? The complaint may be about the boss, a co-worker, the time of day. Whatever it is, if this problem becomes habitual (and it often does), there are a few things you can do to try to stop this vicious cycle in its tracks.

1. Stop it before it starts. If you know that Sharon regularly greets you with a moan about something when you enter her office, or Tony always seems to start complaining to you when you sit near him in the staffroom, simply don't give them the opportunity to continue this habit. Make a point of carrying something with you (memo, letter, notebook, etc.) when you are out and about around the college. Then, if either Sharon or Tony make a beeline for you, politely say, 'Sorry, I'd love to chat, but I have to deliver this,' and walk away purposefully with your piece of paper/notebook in hand.

2. Redirect the complainer. More often than not, complaints are about someone else. Point your complainer in that direction. For example, if it's a payroll related issue that the complainer wants to moan about, tell them that they would get the best result by speaking to someone who has all the right information to hand and can help them – and suggest that they speak to someone in the HR or payroll department. However, if their complaint is about your manager, go to step 3.

3. Ask what they want you to do. Rather than trying to resolve the complainer's issue for them, ask them how you can help. Put the complaint back in their corner for them to decide on their preferred solution.

4. Do not be ignored. In some instances, it may be beneficial to ask the complainer, 'Are you telling me this because you want my opinion or suggestions about what you should do?' If they answer yes, follow this by asking, 'Are you sure, because I know that when I've given my advice or my views in the past you haven't taken me seriously?' At some point you may well be greeted by silence, as the complainer isn't used to being challenged – they are just used to complaining.

5. If they respond that yes, they do want your guidance, give it. Share your insights and tell them that you expect to hear about the positive outcome. They will either steer clear of complaining to you in the future if they don't follow your advice, or they will be happy to share the positive outcome with you and will thank you for the advice you gave.

6. If the answer is no, they do not want your advice or suggestions, tell them, 'In that case, I'm confused about why you want to tell me about your complaint. Unless, perhaps you want me to pass it straight on to the head teacher?' This will give them the chance to back away once more. If they continue talking and complaining, take out a pen and paper, and say, 'Slow down, let me make notes on this, so I can pass on the right information to the head teacher.' Invariably, this will stop them from complaining.

7. If all else fails, tell the person quite plainly, 'You have come to me with complaints several times now. Either you are telling me because you want my advice or because you want me to pass this on to the head, but if you actually don't want either of these, I need to ask you to please walk away and let me carry on with my work – there is no benefit to either of us by you just complaining.'

8. Remind the complainer that the best way to solve an issue is to have alternatives at hand – solutions that resolve the complaint, and that you are encouraging them to try to take this approach.

BRAVERY IS ... RESPONDING TO 'THE CALL'

No, I don't mean hearing a call from God and rushing off to become a nun! I mean the often-dreaded call from the school inspectors: 'We would like to inspect your school and will be arriving at 8 a.m. on Tuesday ...'

Your head teacher or principal will have developed a plan in readiness for this call – who needs to do what, what needs to be done and so on. Remember: your role in supporting them will be of the utmost importance during the visit. This is regardless of whether you are involved in discussions with the Ofsted inspection team or not.

If you are tasked with a role which requires you to meet with the inspection team, you need to be ready and equipped to answer all questions clearly and succinctly. A typical example would be that you may be the person responsible for maintaining the school's single central register, noting all the details of staff, governors, sponsors and regular visitors who have been CRB/DBS checked. Be well prepared for whatever aspects of the visit you are responsible.

A note regarding CRB/DBS checks: the Disclosure Barring System for checking eligibility to work with children and vulnerable adults was introduced to replace Criminal Records Bureau disclosures, but any existing CRB disclosures held by your staff are still valid – there is no 'use by' date on a CRB check. This is despite the rumour that has been around for many years that schools and colleges must renew their CRBs every three years. Ofsted have discouraged this practice and say that it could be seen as mis-use of school funds. They confirm that there has never been a statutory requirement for DBS disclosure certificates to be renewed, except for agency staff or those with breaks in service.[1]

Being able to demonstrate that you have accurate records, in concise, up-to-date, colour coded documents which are stored securely and professionally, is crucial. Keeping calm and unflustered is also key. You might feel nervous, naturally, but if you are well-prepared you can at least alleviate some of your nervousness just by *knowing* that you are well-prepared.

Supporting your head teacher by keeping everything else running smoothly whilst they are meeting with the inspectors is paramount.

If you are not involved in work that requires you to meet with the inspectors, your role will still be extremely important as you will most likely be the person designated to handle any external (and often internal) enquiries to the school whilst your senior leadership team are all busy with the inspectors. Keeping your head teacher or principal supplied with tea or coffee, and maintaining an air of quiet calm in their office, is also vital!

So, before you even get the call, sit down with your boss and talk through with them what you will need to do to support the leadership team in the best way possible. And then get ready – the call can (and probably will) arrive at the most inopportune time!

---

1   Ofsted, Inspecting Safeguarding in Maintained Schools and Academies: Briefing for Section 5 Inspections (January 2015). Ref: 140143. Available at: https://www.gov.uk/government/publications/inspecting-safeguarding-in-maintained-schools-and-academies-briefing-for-section-5-inspections.

BRAVERY IS ... PAPERING OVER THE CRACKS WHEN THE TECHNOLOGY BREAKS DOWN

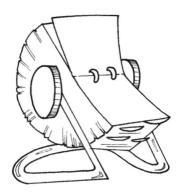

I would like you to imagine a day when you arrive at work and:

- The lights on your desk phone aren't blinking – there are no voicemail messages for you.

- You turn on your computer and your email package shows there are no new messages either from within the college or from the outside world.

- Your college's intranet has stopped and the file storage network is down, so you have no access to any of your work stored on the network.

- The fax machine has stopped receiving or sending faxes.

- You have no internet access so cannot access any files stored on cloud storage.

Can you imagine this?

You might even have to walk down the hall to speak to a co-worker rather than texting them!

You might work in a paperless office environment in your school or college, where almost every piece of paper that enters the building is scanned and digitally stored on a network drive, all filing is held virtually and your office looks like a space-age capsule of tidiness, but there are certain times when you really do need to buck against the system and keep paper records of important stuff.

The students in our schools, colleges and universities have grown up in a world where email and mobile phones are the norm. In contrast, I learned to type on an Imperial typewriter back in the 1980s. When we put an old typewriter in our wonder room (a classroom dedicated to interesting items, with the aim of inspiring learning in different ways), most of the pupils were fascinated by it as they had never seen a real typewriter before. Some even asked what it was!

So how is it that we now rely quite so much upon technology? How did we become so dependent upon it? Undoubtedly, workplace technology has made our lives easier and has improved our working practices and working environment. It's great that offices are no longer cluttered with filing cabinets and our desks are free from the cumbersome Rolodex and the old-fashioned desk diary. This was the world of just a few years ago: this is what we worked with. This is how things were for a long time before the internet and voicemail were created.

But relying too much on technology can lead to problems. The paperless office environment is a great idea in principle, but it must be done with adequate back-up systems and disaster recovery plans in place. If you *only* store important information on your computer and the IT system goes down, a virus crashes your hard drive or the overnight server back-ups fail, the data loss can be catastrophic. (I once worked in a beautiful building next to a river. The whole IT system died because the server equipment was stored on low racks on the ground floor of the building – and the river flooded.) So, it is essential to have a secure and reliable back-up system in place or, alternatively, you might want to consider storing copies of everything on a cloud network.

At times of crisis, your purple folder can come into its own. Once a month, spend just a couple of minutes printing out your contacts list from your email package. Put this printed copy in your purple folder and shred the previous printed version. Once a week, print your boss's diary details and put that in the weekly section of the folder. If nothing else, if your computer system goes down, you will at least be able to telephone the crucial contacts from your list and you can keep track of where your boss should be throughout the week.

Also make sure that you provide back-up files when you create documents for offsite presentations – not only should the files be on the laptop but also on a USB stick. In fact, don't just rely on this for offsite meetings: there is always the chance that, having spent a huge amount of time on a presentation due to take place the following day at your school, you arrive in the morning and the computer network is down so you can't access the files. If you put a back-up copy on a USB stick when you finalise it the night before, all's well and good.

The moral of this chapter: no office can ever really truly be 'paperless', and you should be brave and 'do your own thing' by always keeping an accessible backup of your data.

BRAVERY IS ... ENSURING YOU TAKE TIME OFF!

This might seem an unnecessary chapter for PAs who work term-time only, but for those of you who are on all-year-round contracts it can be of the utmost importance to make sure that you actually take time off.

PAs who have worked in both corporate and education environments report that they found it far easier to schedule annual holidays when working in a corporate environment, despite the fact that most of their colleagues were fighting to take time off during the school holidays in order to spend time with their children. When working in PA roles in education, they found it harder to fit their full allowance of annual leave days into the year. This has often been because they fell into the 'leave tasks until the school breaks for the holidays' trap.

It can be very tempting, in a busy school or college environment, to leave certain tasks for 'during the holidays', reserving them for 'quieter' times when you won't have quite so many interruptions in your office all day, every day. However, not only is this bad planning, because it often means that the task becomes urgent by the very nature of having been left for so long, but it can also lead to you staying at your desk for longer than you need to (because you have to take extra time to refresh yourself with a lot of information from earlier in the term in order to be able to tackle the task now), and it might result in you not taking off appropriate time for *you* during the break.

So, make sure you schedule some time off, and then make sure that you actually take it!

Before you go on your annual leave, it's wise to create a pre-holiday checklist to make sure that you are fully prepared, and to finish up whatever tasks you can before you go – to a reasonable extent. Don't work ridiculously long hours in order to clear *everything* from your desk before you head off for your week on the Costa Blanca or in Skegness ...

Time to call on your 'Bravery SAS' again – you need to remind yourself to put *you* first, so some courage and determination will come in handy here.

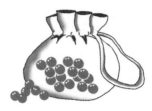

Here are some brave tips for your time-off checklist.

DELEGATE

Delegate some of the tasks that you can't get done to colleagues. If you are a senior-level administrator who supervises other administrators, distribute tasks among them – you will already know who can handle what. If you don't supervise other staff, seek assistance from a colleague you trust, and reassure them that you will return the favour when they go on their annual leave.

Keep a note of what you delegated to whom, which tasks you yourself have completed and which tasks you haven't, and what needs immediate action on your return. There is bound to be more to add to this list of actions when you return, but at least this will give you a starting point and will help you to plan your first week or so after your holiday.

COVER MINOR ASPECTS OF YOUR ROLE BEFORE YOU GO

If your head teacher or principal is going to be in the office while you are away, make sure that you fill up the paper trays on the printers, replace any low toners and order fresh supplies – and let them know where spares are stored and how to change them. It might be second nature for you to pop the printer open, change the toners and clean the print heads, but when your boss is suddenly inkless it's important that they know how to cope on their own! You might also want to leave a list detailing where you keep office basics like staples, pens and folders.

 Believe me, I say this from experience, having received 'urgent' text messages when I was on holiday from bosses in two of my previous jobs, one asking me how to replace the photocopier toner and the other enquiring where the spare teabags were kept!

CALENDARS

Make sure your boss's calendar is up-to-date, and that papers for any forthcoming meetings are in a prominent place, ready for them to take with them. Ask a colleague to keep an eye on the calendar for you – give them a paper copy of it before you go.

TIDY UP

Tidy up your desk space. While you are away things will be put on it by other people, so if you have at least cleared your work out of the way first, this will keep things separate for when you return.

REDUCE INCOMING EMAILS

Without doubt, you will find a very full inbox of emails when you return. There are a few things you can do to alleviate this problem before you go:

- Unsubscribe from any email lists you are a member of, or set your account to 'no mail' on those lists.
- Send fewer emails in the last few days before your holiday – and hence get fewer responses.
- Empty your inbox before you go – file incomplete items in appropriate folders ready to be dealt with on your return.

On your return, allocate yourself a reasonable amount of relatively quiet time to go through the messages that have piled up. Basically, take ownership of your email inbox – don't let it own you!

IN YOUR ABSENCE

- Update your boss last thing before you go on leave to let them know what has been set up to take place in your absence. Schedule a return meeting for when you get back so that you can catch up on what happened when you were away.
- Ensure people know that you are away. Set up an 'out of office' reply on your account that thanks the sender for their message and indicates that you are away and the date of your return. Include alternative contacts should they require immediate assistance. (Put a similar message on your voicemail on both your desk phone and your work mobile phone, if you have one.)

Then head for the hills (or the airport!) …

BRAVERY IS ... SWITCHING OFF YOUR HOME COMPUTER/IPHONE/ BLACKBERRY WHILE YOU ARE AWAY

Following on directly from the last chapter – turn stuff off when you go away!

 For my own part, I used to find this really difficult. I'm a sucker for technology and gadgets and the internet and Facebook and keeping in touch with my friends and reading my email and taking photos and so on ... I would take my smartphone on holiday with me, and connect to free Wi-Fi whenever I found it to upload photos to my Facebook account. I'd then end up checking my personal emails to see if there were any messages that needed my attention, and then I would find myself thinking, 'Oh, and while I'm doing that, I might as well check my work email account too ...'

Many PAs have shared with me what they do when they take annual leave – and it's a common story: many of us spend part of our holiday time doing more work. Does this sound like you too?

I would love to advise you, 'When you go on holiday, put your iPhone or BlackBerry down. Put your hands in the air, and walk away from the Android tablet or iPad. You are on holiday.' It's apparent, though, that this isn't always practical or possible. After spending the rest of the year looking after your boss, it feels perfectly natural to worry that they might need something urgently, so you just do a quick check – and before you know it, you have spent an hour or so of your holiday time on work-related emails.

So, should you or shouldn't you check your emails while you are on leave? These questions remain hot topics judging by recent press coverage. Some PAs are convinced that their bosses need them constantly and that today's 24/7 way of life means that you should be available at all times. Others firmly believe that no one can really switch off properly and get the benefits of being on holiday if they are constantly online, so they wouldn't dream of checking their work email when they are away.

The 2013 UK National PA Survey asked about PA's holiday habits: 'Do you stay in touch with the office when you are on holiday?'[1] The responses were:

- Yes, I check in daily – 14.9%
- Yes, I check in occasionally – 29.5%
- I am available if an emergency arises – 33.6%
- No – 22%

This means that nearly 45% of PAs either phone in, pop in or check their office email accounts when on holiday, whilst a further third are available for emergencies. Only a fifth of respondents said 'no', they kept their holidays completely separate from their work.

So what's the best thing for you to do? It's not just about you making the decision as to whether you log in to your work emails when you are away or not – both you and your head teacher/principal need to be absolutely clear about what they expect of you. It could be

1 Office Show Organiser Announces Results of the 2013 National PA Survey, press release (8 October 2013). Available at: http://www.officeshow.co.uk/office-show-organiser-announces-results-of-the-2013-natonal-pa-survey/.

argued, for example, that you have been given a staff mobile phone expressly so that you *can* be reached at all times, in which case you should perhaps consider leaving the phone at work and organising things so another colleague can cover your role completely when you are away.

Be brave. Set some boundaries.

I would suggest, if you or your boss are really convinced that something might occur that is so urgent that you need to be contacted when you are away, and you truly believe that you can't say, 'No, I will definitely not be available when I'm away,' then strike a happy medium and go for the middle ground. Set up a system with your boss before you go, whereby you give your personal email address to your head teacher and tell them that it can be used in cases of emergency or extreme urgency only. To everyone else – that is, anyone who emails your work email address – you will be unavailable, but your head teacher can reach you if absolutely necessary. However, if you have followed the various tips outlined in the previous chapter, then there shouldn't be any emergencies because you will have fully briefed your boss and a trusted colleague to take on tasks in your absence.

Have a great holiday!

BRAVERY IS ... BACKING INTO THE NUMBER (TO FIND THE RIGHT PATH TO FOLLOW)

Sometimes we might have a task to carry out, but whilst we have an idea of what the finished product should be, we don't have a clue about how to actually get there. If this sounds familiar, here's a great approach that you could use.

If you have ever worked with an accountant you may well have heard the phrase, 'backing into the number'. This is where the end point is known, so everything is geared from that end point. This is a useful method for looking at larger tasks or projects when you feel either overwhelmed or baffled by how to achieve the required aims.

It can also be a fantastic tool to use as a starting point for pretty much everything you do: decide on an outcome and then work backwards to the starting point. So, when you are given a really difficult task, ask the boss what they are seeking as an outcome. Make sure that you spend a few minutes with them on clarifying, defining and refining this outcome so that you can start planning how to tackle the work.

Start from looking at the end product and the last stage prior to completion – what will the project look like when it's almost finished? Then step back in the process once more and look at how to get to the almost finished stage, then one step further back and another … Once you get back to the starting point, pull these together into an outline of a task path through the project, and then review it with your boss to make sure the path you want to follow is both appropriate and correct.

An extremely useful computing tool to assist with any project work is a Gantt chart – a timeline of what needs to be done, when and by whom. You could choose to draw one on paper, but a computerised version gives much more flexibility for moving things around in your project plan and dealing with unexpected hitches For example, if one part of a project ends up running slower than anticipated, you can 'drag and drop' it to a longer timeslot on your Gantt chart, and everything else on the chart should fall into the appropriate new timeslots around it.

To create a Gantt chart, check with your school/college IT department to see if a suitable package is already available via the network, such as Microsoft Project. Alternatively, there are a growing number of free open-source Gantt chart packages that you can find on the internet.

A much simpler version of this approach is the way in which I book my travel arrangements. Let's say I need to source flights for a training course in Geneva. My nearest local airport is East Midlands so it would always be my preference, if possible, to fly from there. My next nearest choice of airport is Birmingham International, then Manchester and then London Heathrow.

I could choose to start by looking at East Midlands Airport's website and checking the list of destinations that I could fly to from there to Geneva. Then, if there are no appropriate flights, I would look at the Birmingham International website to see its destinations, and so on.

Instead, I approach things from the other end – backing into the number, as it were. I visit the Geneva airport website, and see their list of destinations, as this will show me the UK airports that I could fly from and the airlines involved. This is much quicker than spending time looking for flights out of each of my preferred airports. So for some tasks, I'd advocate starting from the endpoint and working towards it.

BRAVERY IS ... JUGGLING YOUR JOB AND YOUR HEALTH

It is so important for you to take care of your own health. For a heck of a long time I didn't. Many PAs join me in this: seeing ourselves as indispensable we battle into work during illness, thinking of ourselves as brave little soldiers and heroically persevering despite being unwell. We go into work because we are so used to being needed in our roles. From having talked with hundreds of PAs on this issue, it's surprising how many of us share this need: a need to feel needed, a necessity to be indispensable to our employers.

However, whilst we might think we are being brave by struggling into work, what most of us are actually doing is prolonging our illness by not allowing our bodies the rest and recuperation time needed to fully recover. Added to this, by continuing to go into work when ill, we're also potentially spreading our germs to everyone else around us, whilst under the misguided apprehension that the world (or at least the school or organisation) would fall apart without us.

On some occasions, we may actually feel a strange sense of satisfaction when we do take a day off and the office seems to fall into chaos – supposedly proving to us that we *are* indispensable and the school can't possibly cope without us.

If you are ill, the bottom line is that you need to think carefully about the importance of your health and realise that there comes a time when you have to say 'Stop!' to yourself. The world will continue to turn if you take a few days off to rest, dose yourself up and give yourself time to get better.

If you are ill and need time to recuperate before returning to work – you *must* give yourself that time.

If you are due to have surgery or other treatment, such that you know in advance you will be off work for some time, don't feel that you just have to suck it up and somehow cope with a huge pile of undone work on your desk when you return. *Be brave* and insist to your head teacher that a plan is drawn up for how things will be handled in your office while you are away. Ideally, either a colleague should move into your role or a temporary PA should be booked to cover your absence – preferably with a handover period of a few days during which you can brief them on the most important aspects of your role that need to be covered. In this way, you shouldn't have to worry about work while you have your

 Sometimes the jolt you need is seeing someone you work with becoming very ill, as I faced with my boss in one role. Until then I had not experienced feeling so worried about a work colleague. When my boss returned to work after a sudden illness, I found myself clucking like a mother hen and trying to protect him more than usual. My stock phrase became, 'You should be going home now ...'

As a result, our working relationship changed in many ways. The main difference was that I became much more aware of him as a person, as a human being with ill health ups and downs, and I found myself asking him daily how things were. I'd never done that before – it had always been a case of 'maintain a professional distance from the boss, don't ask after their health or family'.

Another noticeable change was that I became a lot more wary of my own health issues, and I went to my doctor to insist on being taken seriously about a cough that I'd been suffering from, on and off, for two years. I also urged colleagues to get their own health issues checked. After all, if my boss could go down at the drop of a hat, what guarantee did any of the rest of the staff have that we could stay standing?

surgery or treatment, and you can rest appropriately, secure in the knowledge that your head teacher's world will carry on turning, the school will keep going without you and you can get the rest that you need.

If you are hit with a chronic health problem, you may find that some of your personal priorities change as a result: you may come to value your health far more than you ever did before. Believe me, I know what I'm talking about – but that's another story. I now value what I can and cannot do, and I appreciate what my body allows me to do versus the things that I can't do. My mindset has changed: I'm no longer intent on working myself almost to death in my attempt to be an exceptional PA. Working 'silly hours' isn't the way to be exceptional – instead, the key is finding ways *not* to work silly hours whilst still getting the necessary work done.

Give yourself this opportunity to change your mind about your own health:

- If you are feel unwell, see a doctor.
- If you find something (like a lump) or you have an illness that doesn't clear up after a reasonable amount of time, get it checked out.
- If you are due to undertake a health test of some sort but keep putting it off as you are 'too busy' to have a day-time appointment at your doctor's, make the appointment anyway and go to it.
- If you need to stay in bed for a few days to get over a cold or flu, do it.
- If your doctor says you should take a certain amount of time off, take their advice – do *not* struggle back to work too early as you can make things so much worse for yourself.

I'd urge everyone to check your health. If something's niggling you, get it looked at. Don't leave it until you keel over from something potentially life threatening to make a change.

One major thing has to be noted here: if you find yourself becoming stressed by your job, take some time off. In 2001, the World Health Organization predicted that depression will be the second biggest global burden of disease by 2020.[1] If you are stressed at work, this can build and build until clinical depression sets in. So, if your job is stressful enough to make you sick, or if the pressure of the job is affecting your mental or physical health, your relationships with your spouse or family members, then you need to do something about it. It might be that just a few days away will do the trick, or you may need more time off.

It is not a weakness to recognise and acknowledge that a job can be taking its toll on your life. It is a strength to recognise and acknowledge that actually, you are human, and you need time to rest, relax and recuperate from whatever is making you ill, just like everyone else. If you are stressed by the job to the extent that you wake up dreading the working day, then you need to read page 113 carefully: when you are depressed every Sunday at the thought of the week ahead, it may be time to move on.

Whatever your health problem – get it checked out, get the help you need and take the time off that you need to get better. Take it from me – I know. I've recently gone through a period of ill health and it was only when I gave myself 'permission' to be off work on sick leave that I was able to start relaxing enough to aid my recuperation.

Also remember that whatever illnesses the pupils in your school are suffering from, you are likely to take those germs home with you in the evening and pass them to your own family, or catch the illness yourself. If you've recently returned to work after having a baby and being off on maternity leave, be particularly careful about being around people with infections. Conversely, whatever bugs are in your household could be passed on to others at your workplace.

---

1   World Health Organization, *Mental Health: A Call for Action by World Health Ministers* (WHO: Geneva, 2001). Available at: http://www.who.int/mental_health/advocacy/en/Call_for_Action_MoH_Intro.pdf.

If anyone is off because of vomiting and/or diarrhoea, the rule of thumb should be that they stay away from the school or college for at least an additional 24 hours after they have stopped being sick or their last bout of diarrhoea, in order for the germs to leave their system and not be carried straight back into the school or college.

BRAVE TIPS ON BEING HEALTHIER AT WORK

No one wants to feel sluggish and drained all day, let alone get sick over and over again. Yet, because of the office environment, there are days (sometimes too many of them) where this will be the case. Some preventative steps can help minimise these occurrences.

- Drink lots of water throughout the day. Modern heating and air conditioning systems can lead to dehydration which can affect your energy levels (and attitude). Try to cut down on caffeine: invest in some fruit teas or some decaffeinated coffee for the afternoon, so that you don't go home from work with your mind absolutely racing from too much caffeine.

- Remember to eat – and, no, tea and coffee do not count as a food group! Proper nutrition ensures that your body has the maximum chance to ward off any bugs that may be going around and, again, helps to maximise your performance.

- You probably know what's coming next – get out of your chair and exercise. This can be anything from quick stretches at your desk to a short walk to the water cooler or even a brisk walk around the building or outside.

- And don't forget to breathe! A few deep breaths here and there can help to clear the cobwebs from the brain, send extra oxygen around your system and give you that jumpstart that you need.

BRAVERY IS ... SETTING
SMARTER AIMS FOR YOURSELF RATHER THAN SIMPLY WORKING HARDER

Working harder and harder can be an easy habit to slip into, making it difficult to switch off at the end of the day, take time out at the weekend or stop thinking about work during your spare time.

The aim should always be to make your life easier, not more difficult. My advice in this instance is to make sure that you stay on target towards becoming exceptional in your role by bravely taking charge of your workload and setting yourself SMARTER aims rather than just working harder. SMARTER stands for:

Specific: Make sure your goals are accurate and leave no doubt about what you need to achieve.

Measurable: How will you measure success on this goal? How will you know when it is finished? How will you measure partial success or stages?

Achievable: Giving yourself small goals that are relatively easy to achieve, which together lead to fulfilling a larger goal, is sensible as it is easier to manage small projects and keep them individually on track. Think, 'I have to eat an elephant' – start from one foot at a time. You can't eat it all in one go!

Realistic: Is the goal realistic? Make it relatively easy: the more complicated it is, the more likely you are to encounter problems. Easier goals often mean you can reach them under budget, with good quality results and on time.

Timely: Set a completion date, and be prepared with knowledge of what will happen if you don't achieve your goal by that date.

Evaluate: What has gone well with setting your previous goals, and what went wrong?

Revise/Review: Learn from your mistakes. What have you learned from this process, and what would you change in the future? (See page 45.)

An additional tip for helping you to work SMARTER is to take a breather for five minutes – physically get up and move about, leave the room, make a cup of tea or do some photocopying. Then, when you return to your desk, imagine that you are leaving at the end of the day to go on holiday, and decide which tasks to clear from your action list before you go. It will help you to focus on the things that you *really* need to get done.

The working SMARTER rather than harder principle applies not just to managing and handling your everyday tasks, but also to setting your yearly goals. The ideal time for long-term goal-setting is, of course, your annual performance management review/appraisal, where it is important to remember that everything changes, including goals.

What were your goals this time last year? What are they now? What does your head teacher/principal want you to achieve in the next 12 months? Where do you see yourself, and what do you want to be doing in two years' or five years' time?

Use your appraisal to have a discussion about what both of you would like you to accomplish going forward, and then start setting out your goals on paper (or on screen) to create a realistic plan for the next year – and remember to give yourself as many opportunities as possible to 'work SMARTER not harder'.

BRAVERY IS ... WATCHING
SOME OUT-OF-YOUR-ORDINARY STUFF
ON TELEVISION

You might have firm habits about what you watch on TV, so set yourself the challenge of watching something different for a change. Check out some of the shows that your students enjoy – watch some great stuff, some weird and whacky stuff and maybe something scientific too – ask the pupils for some of their favourite TV shows. And listen to the radio on the way to work every now and again rather than your own choice of music, or to a different station than the one you usually tune in to.

Why? Because it will keep you 'current'. It will give you some shared knowledge of what the pupils and students at your school or college are watching and listening to and some common ground to break the ice with them at lunchtimes. Knowing about the latest episode of a TV show which is popular with the students, or having an idea about what songs are currently in the chart, can give you something to discuss. You can ask if they watched last night's instalment and find out who their favourite person/character in that show is and why.

Many schools now include a panel of pupils during their interview processes for teaching posts. At my school, the pupils always seemed to ask candidates about school-based TV programmes. Candidates would go into the pupil panel interviews, intent on impressing them with their skills and knowledge of teaching, and be stumped when asked, 'Which is your favourite character in *Waterloo Road*?' If the candidate didn't watch it, and couldn't answer the question, then the pupils were not impressed. (I had not watched *Waterloo Road* until I heard some pupils talking about it one lunchtime, but it became standard fodder for the pupil panels during interviews. I think the reasoning on this was to try to gauge what sort of person the candidate was based on their preferred on-screen character.)

So, start watching programmes like *Waterloo Road*, *Educating Yorkshire/Essex*, *The X Factor*, *Britain's Got Talent* and *The Voice*, or perhaps the latest series of *Doctor Who* or about space travel, even if they aren't your usual choice of viewing. This will help to break the ice with students, so you can then engage them in something further.

 I was always interested to hear that some of our more disruptive pupils loved watching school-based shows, even though they purportedly hated being in school themselves. I'd ask them what appealed to them about the TV programmes.

With one pupil, this led to him telling me about his home life, and how sometimes it was better for him to just watch anything on TV (with headphones on) to drown out the arguments in his house. He related to one of the less fortunate pupils in *Waterloo Road* and could see how difficult their life was, and he had great insight into how this affected them at school. This then turned to us talking about how his home life affected him and his behaviour and progress at school.

It was quite an emotional moment for me, hearing this boy of 14 open up about something so close to his heart. I went home that night and ordered a DVD box-set of the first three series of the show so that I could start trying to catch up with it.

BRAVERY IS ... MANAGING YOUR WORKING RELATIONSHIP WITH YOUR BOSS

You need to be behind what your boss stands for. Not every single little tiny thing – you can never be sure of everything they do – but most things, the fundamental things: what they stand for, what they believe in, what their aims and goals are for the school, what their vision is for the future of the college, what changes and innovations they want to bring to the university.

You need to support, respect and believe in your head teacher or principal and what they do. If you aren't in agreement with what they are working to achieve, then I'm afraid you are in the wrong job. How could you possibly provide the best support to someone if you aren't behind them in what they do?

If you find that you only believe in half of what they do, then you must be spending 50% of your time disagreeing with them. That's not going to be conducive to a good relationship or to providing excellent support for them, so my rule of thumb is that you need to endorse at least 75% of what your boss says and does.

In order to provide the best support possible to your boss, you need to believe in them, and by doing this, you can develop a fantastic working relationship with them. This doesn't mean you are going to be 'best buds', but it does mean that you trust each other wholeheartedly and each understands the other.

There are four main stages to your working relationship with your boss.

1. A TELLING RELATIONSHIP

This generally occurs in the early stages of your role, and also in some junior roles, although there are some managers who continue in this vein for much longer. During this phase, your manager will tell you things – they will look at a situation, make a decision, share the outcome with you and tell you what they need you to do.

It is a necessary phase as it informs you of what is needed, to what standard and when. However, it's a stage that you can, and should, grow out of – after a while you should be developing these skills and decision-making processes for yourself. Once you have moved beyond the telling relationship stage, it can feel quite strange to return to it if you change jobs because you will have started to manage your own workload more.

I experienced the telling relationship stage not only early on in my career, but also when I moved country in 2000 and took a temporary contract at one firm where I was one of a team of four PAs, one of whom had been appointed as the senior PA. Regardless of our level of experience, she insisted on doling out work to each of us in a piecemeal fashion, and telling us in great depth what to do with each task. To me, this felt very restrictive after having had much more freedom in my previous roles.

2. AN EXPLAINING RELATIONSHIP

This comes a little further into your working relationship. When your manager trusts you and has taken you into their confidence, they will start to explain to you why they have made certain decisions. This builds your relationship to a more detailed level, giving you much more of an understanding of what is required in your role, including the whys and the wherefores, rather than just being informed that something needs to be done. This can prove very useful when working on a new task or project, when your manager needs additional commitment from you or when they want you on their side to assist in 'selling' an idea to other staff.

This can be a great phase to go through: you will learn a great deal when your boss explains what they mean, how they are thinking and the bigger picture as to where things are going. It's the perfect environment for you to look at your own skills and see what you need to improve in order to fit with the information and understanding that you are now gaining of the organisation. As your working relationship with your manager develops further, it's important that you keep asking questions, finding out more and learning in greater detail. This is what will set you apart from the other administrators in your school, college or university, because you are continually learning about the institution and how your role can make a difference.

I've had some great explaining stages with some of my bosses – helping me to really get to grips with the workings the organisation, and learning how I could make a difference. It's what you do with this knowledge that helps you move on to the next relationship stage.

3. A CONSULTING RELATIONSHIP

This stage brings together the best elements of both you and your manager. It is when they start asking you for your thoughts on various issues, and you make joint decisions together. Reaching this stage with your manager shows that they hold you in great trust, recognise your expertise in what you do and believe that you are working with them in partnership.

 I spent over five years in my most recent role, and for the first year my relationship with my boss was at this consulting stage, before growing further. What I had to say counted for something – and that really mattered to me. It felt liberating, and the working relationship that we had grew from there, into what I felt was a real business partnership.

4. AN EMPOWERING RELATIONSHIP

This is when your manager empowers you to take free rein over what you do and how you handle situations, allowing you to make necessary decisions without consulting them. This requires complete trust on both sides of the working relationship. Your manager has confidence that you have the skills and abilities to handle this level of additional responsibility, and faith that you will represent them and speak on their behalf in the mannerisms and style that they need you to.

 I've reached the empowering level of working relationship with four of my managers throughout my career (the two CEOs during my four years at an international seaport, a deputy vice chancellor at a university and the principal of an academy), and in each of those roles I felt an enormous sense of satisfaction about my work, the level of responsibility that I achieved, the recognition that I received for it and the value in which I was held by my manager. It's a remarkable feeling, and something to really build towards.

It is vital that you see your working relationship with your manager as a two-way street. Whilst you should be aiming to have an empowering relationship with them, the other side of having a great relationship with your head teacher, principal or director requires that you have the courage to speak freely to them on important matters – and not just that they offer you the space to speak. Of course, if you tell your boss something they don't want to hear, they may not want to listen to you. But if you broach the subject with them sensitively, by starting with something along the lines of, 'There's something that I think you need to be aware of ...' or 'May I tell you how I see something?' they are more likely to be receptive to your words.

 From my work with PAs in schools worldwide, I've gathered lots of hints on how to improve working relationships with your head teachers and principals in order to better manage how you work together.

BRAVE TIPS FOR MANAGING YOUR MANAGER

- Empathising. Put yourself in your head teacher's position for a moment: if someone booked back-to-back meetings for you for an entire day, how would you feel at the end of the day? You would no doubt be exhausted, but also you would have had no time to action anything, make phone calls, send emails or pass to your PA any details of work that has come out of those meetings. So, empathise with your head teacher and think about giving them a couple of short 'breathing space' gaps during the day to allow for this. This also provides a buffer for any meetings that overrun slightly, without kicking the rest of the day's schedule off-kilter. Your head teacher may say they don't need these gaps, but believe me, once they've got used to having them they will realise how much they need them to get things done in-between meetings! And for your part, the better you can get to know your head's role, the more you can just go ahead and make the appropriate things happen without them having to tell you, because you have learned to anticipate what is needed.

- Respecting each other. As I've said, it's vital that you support, respect and believe in your head teacher or principal and what they do. Without this, how can you build rapport and support them in running the school or college? Everyone needs some feedback every now and then, so if you respect them, honour what they say, believe in them or find them inspirational, let them know it!

- If in doubt, ask. If you are unsure about something your head teacher has said, ask them for more information. And if, after they have given some more information, you are still in doubt, ask again – ask for it from a different angle so that you can understand how best to support them.

 My office was next door to the principal's office, so he walked through my room to get to his. If I had a visitor in my office and my principal came through to go to his room, I would always introduce them to each other, adding (about the principal), 'He's the most inspiring person I've ever worked for.' It was a completely true statement, and I didn't feel at all embarrassed saying it. Give credit where credit is due, I say!

You can help your head teacher to be more successful by asking thoughtful questions to clarify issues. Never assume and end up making a poor decision because you haven't taken the time or effort or were too embarrassed to get the right information. Remember, you are working in a place of learning, and your head teacher is trained in disseminating information, so they should be able to explain something in a different way for you if you are unclear from their first explanation, and they should welcome that you are checking with them when you are unsure.

- Become a manager yourself. As the head's PA you are in a prime position to develop your own role into that of a manager – working with the school or college's admin team. Ask your head teacher to recommend some leadership and management books and to point you in the direction of useful articles. Consider attending professional development workshops or seminars that could help you to build your leadership skills. Demonstrate to your head teacher that you would like to learn from them how to lead, emphasising that you can help to instil their values and ideals in the admin team based on your close working relationship. Not only does this then mean that the whole team will be working more cohesively, with the same aims, objectives and goals as the head teacher, but it also demonstrates your competence and your commitment to making the school the best it can be.

BRAVERY IS ... KEEPING
GOING – WORKING IN EDUCATION IS A MARATHON NOT A SPRINT

 I've been interviewed by several PA and admin related magazines, most of which are geared towards the corporate world. In every corporate magazine interview, I have been invited to 'Tell us about your average day' or 'Tell us about your average week', to which I had no real answer. The education publications didn't ask me this question – maybe their editors already knew from their own experience that there isn't an average day or week when working in education.

The fact that our working week in a school, college or university is likely to be different every day can be exhilarating. Equally, though, it can be exhausting (and sometimes disheartening) to be confronted with new and different challenges continually.

There are some tasks, of course, that are required of us on a regular basis, but we can often be expected to mop up so many other roles and responsibilities that the constant change can be bewildering for even the most seasoned of PAs.

The fact is that no matter how great your job, how fantastic the people you work with or how inspiring your leadership team, something could happen which means that whatever is good quickly changes to bad, and the results can be ugly.

PAs around the world have related to me that they love that their roles are varied and interesting, but sometimes it can all feel a bit too much, and they wonder how to keep going. I've also heard at length from one PA who, as well as carrying out her own job, was covering the tasks of a colleague who was on long-term sick leave. When her colleague's illness was finally determined to be too severe for her to return to work, the PA was in despair as she couldn't see an end to her doubled role.

There is no point running at full speed from 8.30 a.m. and then falling into a heap at lunchtime with no energy for the afternoon. Working in education is very much like the overall process of children's education – it's not a 100-metre sprint, it's a marathon. We need to maintain a reasonable pace: sustained and steady is far more important than a quick push then having nothing left within us for anything more.

So, when you are tired, overworked or you feel as if you are flagging, reach into your bravery bag and find yourself some encouraging and inspirational beads to help you keep going:

● Winston Churchill gave the best advice of all: 'If you're going through hell, keep going.'

● In *Finding Nemo*, little baby clownfish Nemo makes friends with Dory, the amnesiac fish whose mantra is 'Keep swimming'. No matter how bad things get, or how scary, or how exciting, just keep swimming. Not just treading water on the spot, either – keep actively swimming and moving forward. It's a great mantra for working in a school, college or university environment, where every single day contains completely new challenges and no week is the same as any other.

● For those who remember the 1980s, an alternative mantra might be borrowed from Billy Ocean: 'When the going gets tough, the tough get going'. In other words, don't give up!

So, how do you keep going when things really get bad?

● Concentrate on working on a task until the results are 'good enough', not 'perfect'.

- Adopt planning techniques to divide your tasks into manageable chunks throughout the day.

- Drink plenty of water – your brain needs water to work effectively, but it needs topping up regularly as it does not have any way to store water.

- Take time off on a regular basis – make sure you use up all of your allotted annual leave.

- Make space for you in your free time – space to breathe, think, relax, zone out, whatever you need to do.

 Here are some thoughts from a PA at an international school in Asia about how writing a journal helped her to cope with the stresses and strains of running a business with her husband. She continued with the journal when she moved to her PA role in a school.

I began a journal when we decided to start the business, and I wrote daily about everything that happened in the business – including the good, the bad and the ugly. When I started it, most of the things I wrote about were good, promising, hopeful and exciting. However, as the business grew and we had to make bigger decisions on things like taking on employees, finding new customers and switching suppliers, this created complications.

We found that problems and headaches began to crop up daily, and I ended up spending all of my journaling time writing about the problems, just the problems. I continued writing the journal during our ten years in business and it was really useful to look back on when we had a really difficult problem to solve in the business, as the journal showed how my husband and I had managed to overcome similar or harder issues in the past. Time and time again, I realised we had both been in hell for several years in that business and worked our way through it.

Now, working in a school, I continue to keep a journal for the same reason – to show myself and others that if I can do it once, I can do it again. And if I can do it, so can you.

Cecilia, Singapore

Start writing daily in a journal now. It will remind you that you have what it takes to be successful, even when your head doubts it. You will also learn not to make the same mistake more than once and be better prepared for future obstacles.

BRAVERY IS ... ANSWERING CALLS FROM PARENTS

One of the most daunting things during a school day can be answering calls from angry or upset parents and family members, particularly if they are making demands that you can't immediately fulfil, like 'I want to speak with the head teacher *right now*' (but he's physically out of the building) or 'My child *must* be given a place at your school because of X, Y or Z' (but there are 20 other children on the waiting list for places who are deemed, by the entrance criteria, to be higher in the rankings for a place than this particular child, if one becomes available). Even more scary is the physical presence of a distraught parent in the school's reception area yelling, 'I'm here, I want this sorting out *right now.*'

As PA to the head of the school, we are often the person in the front line, the person who needs to deal with these calls and visits while the head is in a meeting, off-site or otherwise engaged. If you have the right skills, you can be an excellent line of defence when it comes to taking calls or visits from angry or upset parents or members of the local community. You can diffuse situations and take care of matters before they need to be escalated to a teacher or the head of the school.

It helps to develop your listening skills, and be able to give the necessary space for someone to be heard. It is also sensible for you to know and understand the school or college's policies and procedures regarding poor behaviour, bullying, cyber-crime, grievances, homework and so on, so that you can explain these in laymen's terms to parents. Sometimes just explaining the school's rules on an issue can solve the problem without anyone else having to get involved. Once the parent realises that what their child has done is against the school's rules or policies, they will often accept this and you can move forwards more easily.

Knowing the next steps in the school's process for complaints is paramount, so that you can use the correct system and the right chain of command to take the complaint further. It may be that the parent has come straight into the school and is demanding to see the principal, but the issue is actually the responsibility of their child's head of year, and the school's procedures state that this particular matter needs to be passed to that member of staff to deal with. Then, and only then, if the parent is unhappy with how it has been dealt with should they then see the principal. Being able to explain to the parent that the school has a process for dealing with complaints, so that the right people are involved at the right level throughout, can be useful.

Making sure that your receptionists are well-versed in the complaints procedure is vital too – to ensure that they contact the appropriate member of staff to come to reception to see a parent or put a call through to the right office. No matter how difficult the situation, we should maintain a warm and welcoming attitude to our pupils' parents and the community, and always give them the best first impression we can. It is helpful when recruiting new administrative staff to look for caring and calming individuals, because any one of them might have to answer a call from, or be greeted by, an upset parent.

Keep in mind that the angry or upset parent in your office or on the telephone has very likely heard only one side of the story and is reacting to this. Many parents want to believe that the words of their children are the truth, the whole truth and nothing but the truth. As a result, they can often react without full knowledge of all of the details, which is why it is important for you to ascertain what they know and who told them, in order that you (or another staff member) can find out what else happened and why.

Your aim should be to demonstrate to parents that their child is important to you and that you fully understand their concerns. Showing this empathy and understanding can help the parent to calm down so that you can have a useful conversation with them about resolving the issue.

So, how are you going to do this? Pick up your bravery bag and root around in it for some calmness and a sense of helpful authority. These are the main skills you need to use, along with the knowledge that, for the vast majority of issues, the parent is not complaining about you personally. Remember the mantra: it's business, not personal.

A great approach to use when dealing with upset parents is TO LEAP towards them:

Thank them for coming in or for calling, and tell them that it is good to know they are passionate about their child's education. Thank them for informing you about their concerns/issues and reassure them that you will do all you can to help.

Open/Offer the door to your office and invite them to come in and sit down, or offer your time on the phone. A good thing to say is, 'Hold on, let me just put a sign on my door so we won't be disturbed, so that you can have my full attention.' This assures them that you are going to give them time and will be listening to them fully. Whilst you are doing this, it also gives you the opportunity to quickly ask a nearby staff member to take your other calls. You may also get the added benefit that the few seconds of separation will allow the angry parent to calm down a little.

Listen. When parents are upset, they want to be heard. Many seem to think they must raise their voice to be heard. So listen, actively! Take in what they are saying. Repeat it back to them to indicate that you have heard and understood the issues.

Empathise. Indicating that you understand why they might feel angry or upset about an issue – even if you think they are wrong or misguided – is the key to moving things forward. You are empathising with them and acknowledging that their feelings are real. Let them know that you can see/hear that they are upset, and say something like, 'I'm sorry this is so upsetting,' 'I'm sorry you feel that we made a wrong decision' or 'I see you are very upset, and I would be too if this had happened to my child.' Then add, 'You are right to bring this to us – thank you.' All of these statements reassure the parent that you are listening to their complaint.

Ask intelligent and useful questions like, 'Can you give me the full details of what has happened?', 'Is this what your child has told you or what you have heard from a teacher/someone else who was there?', 'Who else might have seen/heard this, so we can double check what happened?' or 'Is there anything else we should be looking into?' If the issue is about their child's alleged behaviour in school ask, 'What are they like at home?' or 'Does what you have heard today sound like them normally?' Asking questions like these can help the parent to feel that you care and that you are concerned about resolving the issue. It suggests that their feelings and viewpoint are valued. It may well be that the parent is shouting and becomes aggressive, but calmly asking questions, and being seen to take notes on what they are saying, can help to diffuse the anger as you are demonstrating that you are taking them and their concerns seriously.

Problem-solve/Plan/Promise. Ask the parent, 'What do you want me to do to help towards fixing this?' or 'What do you think we should do from here?' Quite often they will have no answer to this, but you are giving them an opportunity to have an input into what happens next. Depending on the issue, you might be able to solve the problem yourself, or it might be that it needs to be passed on to another member of staff, possibly even the head teacher or principal. Either way, put forward a plan to the parent as to what you intend to do – who you are going to talk to and what is likely to happen – and make sure that you promise to get back to them as soon as possible to report on the next steps/stages/resolution.

A word of caution: try to stay calm if a discussion becomes heated. Keeping on even keel often disarms agitated parents and can lead them to becoming more calm and rational.

However, if a caller or visitor is aggressive and they refuse to calm down, if they use profanity or if you feel in any way physically threatened, be brave and quietly explain that you have to stop the conversation until they have calmed down – and remove yourself from the situation. In other words, stop the call/conversation and get out. Put their call through to a senior member of staff or get up and walk out of the room. It is not brave to accept abuse or to feel threatened – you have the right to feel safe at work and to expect a certain standard of acceptable behaviour.

BRAVERY IS ... ADAPTING YOUR PLANS QUICKLY AND DEVELOPING ALTERNATIVES

Always be ready for sudden changes!

Imagine you've got a VIP coming to your school or college. Everything is ready – you know when they are arriving and who is coming with them, there is a programme of events in place and you have groups of staff and students standing by – and then you get one of the following phone calls:

> 'I'm afraid there's a horse loose on the M25 so the traffic is completely at a standstill. We will be late for the Grand Opening.'

> 'The royal helicopter is delayed in landing because of fog. The whole programme for the day will have to be put back – maybe by an hour, maybe more. We don't know yet.'

What do you?

First of all, inform the head teacher or principal as soon as you possibly can, and start drawing up new plans. A good PA plans the VIP visit; a brave PA is ready to adapt everything quickly when things happen beyond your control!

If a visitor has been delayed, your head teacher or principal should be able to come up with some alternative arrangements. You will probably be required to carry out most of this work and to disseminate information to the rest of the team. This might involve quickly editing some PowerPoint slides for a presentation, briefing staff members, holding off the catering team from serving food for an undetermined period and liaising with the local press.

On a more day-to-day basis, some slightly less high profile changes to schedules and events will almost certainly be required – for example, it is almost inevitable that a last-minute meeting will come up just as you are about to leave the office. It is very likely that your head teacher or principal will need you to be available for emergencies like this. Good time management should help you to organise things smoothly at this point – and you can reassure your boss that you are on top of things. A great PA will always double check (and sometimes even triple check) each of the calendar entries to ensure accuracy and to avoid an important meeting being missed.

When organising any travel plans, take charge of the itinerary and make it your task to inform everyone involved as soon as there are changes. Your time management skills will be required, especially if the travel requires crossing time zones as there will be time differences involved. If, like I did, you work for someone who goes abroad on international trips as a speaker at education events, I'd advise that you make an effort to clear some space in your own diary to match those trips. This means that if your head teacher experiences a problem while they are away, you are available by phone/email and have time to fix whatever has gone wrong, or to create a new report or presentation to forward to them on their travels.

Remember: a brave PA is also a flexible PA (we're the Olga Korbut of the working world!). We need to be able to adapt and change, to pick up and carry on and, most of all, to not panic. (Think of yourself as a swan gliding across a lake: from above the waterline you see a beautiful serene swan. From below the waterline, all you can see is the swan's legs thrashing around in the water. You might like to try to keep this in mind in your office when all hell suddenly seems to break loose and a panic occurs!)

BRAVERY IS ... WELCOMING CRITICISM (AND SOMETIMES BITING YOUR LIP)

The boss nodded his head around my door: 'Angela, could you just pop in for a moment so I can have a word?'

 Earlier in my career, I hated hearing this as I equated 'having a word' with my having done something wrong and there being a telling off on its way. And I was usually right: something I'd done had gone awry or something I'd said had been off-kilter with someone else's view, and I'd then be told what I'd done wrong, who'd taken umbrage against it or how it had affected a project or a piece of work, and what to do about it.

I would sit there in the boss's office, red faced with shame, feeling inadequate, silently kicking myself and mumbling apologies. I would walk out of the office feeling like I was completely useless, telling myself I would never do whatever it was again.

In more recent years, though, whilst I still cringed inwardly at the invitation to go into the boss's office for them to 'have a word', and I still felt some shame at having done something that had been perceived as wrong, I started to embrace the learning that resulted from the error.

I stopped saying to myself that I wouldn't do it again. Instead, I joined in the conversation with my boss to discuss what other options I could have used, working out how I could resolve this sort of issue in the future and listening to the message behind it all: my good intentions and my integrity were not in question. It was not a fault in me as a person, it was something that I had done which could be rectified and worked on.

I'm not saying for one minute that I enjoy having an error pointed out to me – I don't think anyone does – but it is important to be able to develop the type of working relationship with your manager which enables you to talk *together* about issues. There is no need to just sit there, feeling exposed to criticism and unable to do anything about it. Criticism is one of those things that's hard to take, but over time it's better to have it than not to have any comments at all about how well you are doing. I used to dread it; now I look for it. I ask the attendees on my training courses to complete feedback forms, and to be honest when doing so. (I also add, 'Be honest, but not brutal, please!' to encourage them to give constructive criticism.)

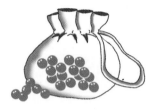

TRANSFORMING CRITICISM INTO A USEFUL LEARNING AND DEVELOPMENT TOOL

 Many of the PAs I meet on my training courses describe working for managers who seem to criticise them all the time or who never seem to have a word of praise for them. When they ask me what to do, I share Jenny's story with them. She is a PA in an international school in the Fast East, who has experienced working for a boss who made her feel like this (she gave me permission to tell her story to others).

Jenny worked for three members of her school leadership team – two who praised her now and then for her work, but the third one only ever seemed to criticise her. Unfortunately for Jenny this was the person who was responsible for carrying out her yearly appraisal. During the first few years of working at the school the appraisal meetings were miserable affairs: Jenny felt that she was being told off for the entire time.

As she grew within her role, however, Jenny noticed that the two directors who praised her only ever gave praise to her – there was never any negative feedback at all. As Jenny observed, 'I knew I wasn't perfect and I knew I made mistakes sometimes, but either they never seemed to notice or they didn't care, so their praise started to mean nothing to me.' This insight helped her to realise that the third director, the one she had thought of as highly critical, was actually the person who was helping her to develop most within her role, pushing her to become better at certain things, leading her towards a higher level of working. She added, 'I started to realise that criticism can be useful, so even when I felt that maybe the criticism I was receiving was a bit too harsh at times, I looked at it differently, trying to work out how best to use it to improve myself and my work.'

Jenny also started to challenge the two directors who only ever praised her work. She said to them, 'Please let me know if I do something wrong or that you are not happy with. I'd welcome your thoughts, and you are not going to "break me" or upset me if you tell me there's something that you'd like me to do better.' She now feels that she has a more respected standing amongst her colleagues and feels much happier about work in general.

Being able to hear critical comments, even to invite them when they are not forthcoming, and to work on them to your advantage is a great skill to acquire. It is also one of the hardest – after all, no one likes to hear bad things about themselves. But it can be an incredibly useful learning tool: if we take apart the criticism that we receive and break it down into manageable parts we can build on it.

'IT'S BUSINESS, IT'S NOT PERSONAL'

Being able to separate out the emotional aspect from criticism is a key aspect, so use your emotional intelligence and remember, 'It's business, it's not personal'. The vast majority of criticisms you receive about your work will be about the ways in which you work, how you have done something or what you have said – not about you as a person.

LEARNING HOW TO GIVE CONSTRUCTIVE CRITICISM TO OTHERS

Learning to give criticism (or 'constructive feedback') to others is something that you'll develop over time. For example, you might be managing a project and need to steer a team member in a particular direction when they have gone off course, or you might be responsible for the office team and need to speak to someone about the quality of their work which has gone downhill sharply.

Another example where this is really important is providing feedback to service providers. Say, for example, you spend two or three days attending a training course, and at the end of it the trainer presents you with a feedback form to fill in. Aim to give some constructive feedback. If the form has tick boxes for you to show how useful the various sessions were and boxes for comments, I would urge you (as a trainer now myself) not to just tick the boxes to say it was 'very good', 'good', 'average' or 'below average', and leave the rest of the form blank. Whilst the tick boxes are good overall gauges for the effectiveness of a training course or seminar, the person receiving the feedback will also want some information from you about what was good, what was average and what fell below par. Good feedback forms should give you space to include some comments, so use this to really give your views on how it's been for you.

If your manager said to you at the end of the week, 'I'm giving you 3 out of 5 for this week,' and then said nothing more, you would want to know why you didn't get a 4 or 5, or what you could change so that you could get a 4 or 5 in the future, wouldn't you? Also, don't be ambiguous – 'I really enjoyed the course' doesn't communicate what you enjoyed exactly. What did you enjoy? Being away from the office for two days? Learning in a conducive environment with a great trainer? Meeting other people in similar roles? Having time to snooze on the back row? The great lunches and snack breaks? Put in some detail.

You can use this same approach when giving feedback or criticism to colleagues. By all means give marks on a scale to be measured against in the future, but back up your marks with specific useful comments on what was good, what was bad and what can be improved upon.

 In the last five years, I have worked with more than 2,500 personal assistants, executive assistants and administrative staff. Part of my learning curve within this time has been to recognise that it can be hard to get useful feedback at the end of a course because the attendees are tired, full of ideas (hopefully) and ready to go home. Quite often, they would just tick the boxes on the form and leave. For me as the trainer, though, this is my major opportunity to gain some insight into how well the course has gone, whether the work was pitched at the right level for the audience, whether the handbook and presentations were up to the expectations of the group and how or why particular sections of the course seemed to go better or worse than others.

On the most recent training courses I've delivered, I've now started to include a short session on giving and receiving feedback within our jobs, and the importance of being able to take and give constructive criticism – and *then* I've handed out the feedback forms and asked the attendees to put this session to use. As a result, the comments I've received have been much more enlightening for me as a trainer, enabling me to build their thoughts into the next iteration of the course. I intend to use this session in every course from now on.

BRAVERY IS ... FEELING
YOUR WAY THROUGH THE FEAR

It has to be said at some point: it can feel scary, disconcerting, uncomfortable or downright unpleasant when we are being brave, but it can be *so* worth it. Sometimes we just need to stand up, bite the bullet and take it on the chin (you may wish to insert your own choice of metaphor here) in order to combat something that scares us. In this chapter we'll look at two particular instances in your role where you will definitely need to dig deep into your bravery bag for your courage, determination and leadership skills: leading a team for the first time and combating bullying in the workplace.

MANAGING A TEAM

At some point in your career as a PA you may be given the responsibility of managing a team of administrative staff. If you have never been responsible for other members of staff before, welcome to your own personal episode of *Fear Factor*! It can be scary to lead a team for the first, second, third or tenth time. Not because you don't have the skills to deal with whatever comes your way – undoubtedly, as a PA in a busy school, college or university you have all the skills you need within your toolkit – but because it can take such an enormous amount of tact and diplomacy to lead a team, and such a lot of effort to motivate, encourage and cajole.

So, how would you bravely tackle the following scenarios?

- Trying to persuade a colleague (who thinks they are 'doing well enough, thank you') to attend a training course because you can see that their knowledge or skills are lacking in some way. How would you broach this in order to keep the colleague on side and motivate rather than offend them?

- Working with another colleague who is very easily distracted by technology to persuade them not to spend every moment at work trying out new things on their computer, but to find a gentle balance between learning and getting things done, and all the while trying not to crush their sense of purpose at learning something new. After all, we want our colleagues to be developing within their roles, but not to the detriment of failing to get the work done.

- Being the 'young office manager' with responsibility for a team of staff who are older than you and who have been with the organisation for far longer than you. It can be scary to take charge in this kind of situation and to exert a level of firm but calm authority.

I can't teach you all the leadership skills you might need in this one chapter – that would be a separate book entirely. What I will advise is that you listen to and learn from those around you – your senior leadership team, your head teacher or principal, the teachers or lecturers on the staff. See how they get things done and how they persuade others to do things in certain ways.

COMBATING BULLYING IN THE WORKPLACE

Another example of where you are going to need some real bravery is handling bullying – either if you are the person being bullied or if you are trying to assist someone else who is. It can be really distressing to be the person who is being bullied, but it can also be very difficult to help someone else who is being bullied, and to urge them to lodge a formal complaint when necessary.

Some workplace bullies are very quiet about what they are doing, keeping it between themselves and the person they are mistreating. Others bully everyone and anyone. (I worked with the latter sort of bully in the early stages of my career – a woman who shouted at colleagues, both those above and below her in the organisation's hierarchy, and thought nothing of it. She was frightening – she blew up into loud angry rages, slammed things about on her desk, huffed and puffed, and went red with anger.) How would you deal with working with someone like that?

Knowing when to stick up for yourself or others, and when to take something further to higher management, can be difficult. How do you gauge what is 'bad enough' to take forward as a formal complaint, for instance?

You will find, over time, that you will develop your own moral compass, a code by which you operate, where you know and recognise the levels of what is acceptable and what isn't, and what needs to be reported higher. But learning your own code and finding your way through it at the start can be very scary. It is at times like this that you will find yourself dipping into your bravery bag to find the various skills within you to help you combat bullying: your morals, your ethics, your feelings of right and wrong and your sense of justice will all come into play. Each person has their own moral compass, we're all slightly different.

Quite often, a workplace bully has other problems than just the clearly visible anger issues – bullying often stems from cowardice or fear of some sort. (In the instance of the bully I met early on in my career, she was very insecure about her position in the job. In the time that I worked with her, I could see that there were certain tasks that she seemed unable to complete or, at the very least, was reluctant to take on. She would farm these items out to me or to another colleague rather than attempt them herself, but on the couple of occasions when she could not do this she seemed more than usually flustered, and mistakes were later pointed out in her work.) Bullies will use their anger and frustration at their own shortcomings to keep other people at bay, often in an attempt to ensure that nobody bothers them with tasks that they are unable to carry out, and to prevent themselves from being 'found out' as lacking in some way.

I think it's human nature that people do not wish to be perceived as weak in any way, so some of your colleagues may seem to prefer to be bullied by someone at work than to put in a complaint that they are being bullied. It's a very complex situation – one which needs careful handling, especially if you are the office manager and are responsible for one or more of the members of staff involved.

There's also the possibility that you might be the person on the receiving end of the bullying – from a co-worker, from someone in your college leadership team or even from your boss. Standing up to bullying is intensely hard on the person being bullied.

BRAVE TIPS ON HANDLING WORKPLACE BULLYING

Could you confront a workplace bully? Here are my tips:

- Pick an appropriate moment to talk to the bully – and keep in mind that you need to keep your cool, so that you can speak with them clearly and directly.
- Speak with the bully in private and away from prying eyes or listening ears. It should certainly be away from any of their supporters (if they have any); most bullies are cowards and without their supporting pack you have more chance of getting your point across.
- Work out beforehand what you want to say to them – know where their actions and behaviour have contravened your school/college anti-bullying policy. If need be, run through a practice conversation in your head beforehand and have notes with you to ensure that you can cover what you want to say without missing anything.
- Make sure you have specific examples of their behaviour to talk about, not just 'You are bullying Miss Smith.' Instead, be able to

say something more detailed like, 'We need to talk about what happened in the corridor on Monday morning when I saw and heard you shouting at Miss Smith.'

* Make sure that you add something along the lines of, 'We need to work with each other respectfully, so let's talk about how we can improve our communication with one another.'

Not confronting a bully allows them to get away with their behaviour. Speaking up lets them know that you are holding them accountable for their actions and that you are serious about putting a stop to their behaviour.

At the very least, the hope is that your speaking up will prompt a change in their pattern of behaviour. Yes, it's going to feel scary doing it, but knowing that you are working to stop unacceptable behaviour can give you a boost of self-respect and self-confidence.

If we choose not to do anything about workplace bullying, what sort of example are we setting to our students? It is only by addressing bullying head-on that we will be able to make a difference and stop it. Don't let fear of a bully prevent you from doing something about it, or allow bullying to push a member of staff (including yourself) to leave their job because the bullying is too much to deal with. Be brave and stand up for yourself and your colleagues.

BRAVERY IS ... ACKNOWLEDGING IF YOU ARE NOT FEELING FULFILLED – AND DOING SOMETHING ABOUT IT

ENJOYING YOUR WORK IS IMPORTANT IN BEING AN EXCEPTIONAL PA

Once a year or so, usually around the beginning of the new school year or just after New Year's Day when we are busy making resolutions towards being a 'better' person, we have a tendency to want to take stock of our lives: where we've been, where we are, where we're going. Finding contentment at work is probably high on our list – and, yes, it is possible.

Here are some brave tips for how to make your job more enjoyable.

LEAVE HOME AT HOME

You already spend enough time at home worrying about home items, such as the house, the kids, the bills and so on. Dragging this baggage into work is not only unfair to you, but also to your employer. So leave your personal issues at home where they belong. This may be easier said than done – the trick is to find a way to shut the door on the problem when you walk into the office. If you are having trouble, seek out a friend who might be able to shed some light on your situation and offer some advice on how to separate the two.

ENJOY YOUR SURROUNDINGS

How many hours a day do you spend at work? Too many, right? Well, regardless of your actual work space – whether your desk is in your own office or in an open-plan environment – make the space your own. The goal is for your workspace to feel both relaxing and motivating. Seem impossible? Well, it's not as hard as you might think. According to Brenda, a HR manager at a school near Boston in Lincolnshire, 'You don't want to decorate as if this were your home. Instead, you want to personalise the space with such things as photos and small items that mean something to you. Find a combination of items that you can either look at or hold when you are either feeling stressed or seeking to recharge your battery.'

DEVELOP FRIENDLY RELATIONSHIPS

While work is not supposed to be a place to socialise, it is where you spend the majority of your time, so it only makes sense that you should have a friendly face or two that you can call on. These can be relationships that stay at work – it can be as simple as just having coffee for a few minutes each day or as involved as eating lunch once a week. The key is to find someone you can lean on for support, and who you can offer support to in return, without worrying about what is discussed being made public.

CHAOS CREATES CHAOS

Disorganisation is one of the most frustrating things at work. The main reasons for this are quite simple: either you have no time to get organised or you don't have the skill set to be effective at it. So, here's a quick three-step approach to stopping the chaos.

1. Make one pass at everything on your desk or in your office and apply the 'touch it once rule'. You must (a) throw it out, (b)

delegate it or (c) act on it. During this first pass, the goal is to unclutter and get all the 'act on it' items in one place.

2. Select one item to act on and follow it through to completion. We sometimes have so many projects overwhelming us that we start this, and dabble on that, and fiddle with this, and yet nothing gets finished. Experience what it feels like to get one thing accomplished.

3. Be realistic in what you can and cannot do. It's surprising how much work you can get done when you set a time frame for completing it. This typically happens before you are about to take your annual leave when you make extreme, rash and sometimes exceptional decisions about a task because you have something more important (and usually better) that you want to do. Try taking control over a 30 minute period before lunch each day and pretend (in your head) that you are not coming back after lunch. Get everything done that you possibly can, by using tremendous focus during that 30 minutes.

FIND ACCEPTANCE

A trend seems to have arisen in which employees find it's their job to 'flag' their peers who are being either ineffective, inefficient or both. Granted, this is usually driven by frustration because of a specific incident (e.g. you are depending on someone to give you a paragraph of text and they don't, and this now means that your report is late, which will result in further problems with sending out papers for a meeting). Instead of waiting to be let down by others, accept that sometimes there are going to be delays from certain quarters which you can do nothing about. Plan ahead for the unexpected, and develop a system for going around obstacles.

REWARD YOURSELF

You may work and work and work, and all you achieve may go completely unnoticed. This can be quite demotivating, to say the least. However, you are at your job to work, not to receive pats on the back. So, set a personal goal for yourself and reward yourself for achieving it. This could be a nice lunch or a trinket for your desk.

STAY POSITIVE

You can't hear this often enough – stay positive. One of my favourite song lyrics is, 'We've got two lives: one we're given and the other one we make'.[1]

Your outlook on life is entirely up to you. Make an active decision to try to see the positive in the world around you and in all aspects of your job: compliment a colleague, email a note of appreciation to someone else's boss, thank someone who helped you with a project, invite a new staff member to lunch. These are all little things that can have a tremendously positive impact. Try just one a day, and see what happens!

---

1   Mary Chapin Carpenter, 'The Hard Way' (1993).

FEELING FULFILLED IS HIGHLY IMPORTANT IN BEING AN EXCEPTIONAL PA

If you aren't sufficiently challenged or satisfied with your role, either work towards making it more fulfilling or move on.

We all need to feel fulfilled in our work if we are to truly excel in what we do. It might be that you get up each morning, go to work, do a good job, make some decent money and possibly even enjoy yourself, but deep inside something is missing. You might feel that your job isn't worthwhile, or you aren't working to your full capacity, or you aren't finding it as challenging or it isn't as interesting as you would like, and this prevents you from giving the best of yourself. You might feel trapped or you might feel that whilst your salary meets what you need to run your home, you are not happy. You might feel that, even though you are successful in your role, you don't get the creative spark you need. If you don't feel emotionally fulfilled or socially content, you can end up feeling stuck or discouraged. All of these are signs that you need to change something within yourself, change something within your job or actually change job.

This may all sound like doom and gloom – and if you do feel unfulfilled, you join the millions of people in industries the world over. There is good news though – there are ways to fix this.

You should always consider talking with your boss and explaining that you are seeking something more satisfying or demanding from your job. You may decide not to, of course, but if you are confident about asking for new challenges, then let them know that you are looking to feel more fulfilled, more useful or more successful in your role. Your head teacher may not have realised that there was a problem, or may have seen that you have been unhappy but not known what to do about it. A good boss will welcome the opportunity to develop your role or to give you some additional or different responsibilities. To prepare yourself for this talk, you might want to think about the following pointers.

KNOWING AND APPRECIATING WHO YOU ARE

Be happy with who you are. Know what your capabilities are, acknowledge your gifts and your talents, and decide how they could be used in a better or different way. Make a list of the things that you do well and celebrate them. Remember that you bring special assets to the table, so work on defining what you can do with them.

DON'T TRY TO BE SOMETHING YOU'RE NOT

Often we try to fit ourselves into the ideal of what we believe or think others want or expect of us, but frequently our assumptions are wide of the mark. Quite apart from trying to mould ourselves into something we're not, this can disconnect us from who we actually are. Don't suppress your gifts and talents. Don't stay in a job that doesn't fit your ambitions, where you feel unfulfilled or where you suspect your talents are not required or your skills are being wasted. Look deep inside yourself to see if you should be doing something else. Working as a PA or an administrative assistant within a school, college or university is an incredibly busy and hard-working job. But if it doesn't feel right for you, acknowledge that. If you want to take on more responsibility within your role, make a list of possible areas you'd like to work in – and then get on with doing it! This applies, of course, to every job – not just working in education – but sometimes it can take real bravery to acknowledge, accept and do something about not being fulfilled in your job. Don't just sit and moan to yourself that it doesn't feel right, or that you don't fit in, or that your role isn't satisfying.

BE TRUE TO YOURSELF

You don't only need to accept who you are – you need to honour that you are who you are. Don't compromise. Be proud of your accomplishments. By remaining true to yourself, you are more likely to find the area you want to work in because you will have the necessary self-confidence. You are likely to be more appealing to prospective new employers, or to your boss when you suggest changes to your role, because your self-belief will shine through.

DON'T BE AFRAID TO DREAM

Many people are unwilling to allow themselves to dream of a career where they feel fulfilled and have a sense of accomplishment. But these jobs *do* exist – and I hope your role can become one of these! I remember seeing a cartoon once in which a man sat on a park bench saying to himself, 'There must be more to life than sitting around thinking there must be more to life.' And I thought, 'How sad to have nothing to dream about.' Write a list of the things you love and are passionate about. Look at the list and try to decide for yourself what you really want to do. At this point, don't try to fit it into a specific career, industry type or area – just reflect on your overall dreams and where they fit with your passions. Then look at how you might possibly incorporate these into your existing role or where they might be available within other roles.

LET GO OF THE FEAR OF CHANGE

Many people hold themselves back from new ventures because they are terrified of change. Sometimes just changing your mind can be all it takes to open up the possibility for new opportunities. Fear can be a strong motivator to staying still, remaining stuck and not moving on. Ask yourself if not facing your fear is holding you back. If so, let go of it and see what happens. Embarking on something new – like starting a training programme, becoming involved in an after-school club where you would be working in a very different way with pupils and teachers or creating a new CV after many years of working in one role – can feel very unnerving, but just think about how much enjoyment you could get from embracing the change, pushing through the uncomfortable period and moving into a more challenging (or more restful) and fulfilling future.

BRAVE UP AND FACE THE RISKS

It would be foolish to imagine there are no risks involved in changing job, employer, profession or industry. By nature, most of us are realistic and level-headed, so we recognise there may be unforeseen consequences. Progressing towards your desire to be fulfilled in your work doesn't mean that you have to give up everything you know. Yes, there will be risks, but you need to work out what risks those are and which ones you are willing to take. The choice is yours.

DON'T JUST SIT THERE – GO FOR IT!

Defining their dream is sometimes where many people stop. Thinking about the time and effort that will be involved in making changes to your job, hunting for a new job, making the necessary plans to take a training course or pushing yourself towards a different career can feel intimidating.

You can conquer this by making a step-by-step plan and then following it. Your plan could involve researching or talking with a mentor about your desired aims – either within your current role or a new one. Consider letting the appropriate people know that you are searching for something new. For example, if you would like to move into a project management role, you could indicate this to your boss and to others within the school or college, to people within your networks and to others who work in project management roles elsewhere. Set yourself targets for learning more about your desired goal or preferred profession for the future.

So, start taking action and working towards your goal. Just having an ambition is not enough: you need to act on your dreams. The end result will be well worth it, and you will be pleasantly surprised at what you learn about yourself in the process.

BRAVERY IS ... PUSHING YOURSELF BEYOND YOUR LIMITS AND PUTTING YOURSELF FORWARD FOR SOMETHING OUT OF THE ORDINARY

This chapter is not about insisting that everyone reading this book must undertake a parachute jump for charity, run a marathon or push themselves beyond all reasonable limits to gain some extra brownie points for doing something extraordinary. 'Out of the ordinary' does not have to mean 'extraordinary' – it can just mean something that you wouldn't do, or wouldn't be expected to do normally in your role.

This might sound uncomfortable – asking you to do something you wouldn't normally do. However, think back to times when you have been taken out of your comfort zone in your own school or college years or in another job – perhaps having to deliver a presentation on an unfamiliar topic or taking the lead on a project when you hadn't been given that kind of responsibility before. You will probably discover you had the bravery to do it all along.

Here are just a small number of examples that could be included in this category:

- You might like singing, so why not suggest to the music teacher that the school choir should also include staff, and put your name down? (For example, I worked with the students who ran our school's own record label. I got really involved by going through the process of creating my own single, and I found that I loved the experience so much that I ended up applying to go on *The X Factor* and then sharing my experiences with the pupils!)
- Maybe you have great skills with make-up, painting scenery or making costumes, so why not put your name down on the list for getting involved in the annual school performance?

- Do you have a skill or art that you could teach in a one-hour-per-week timeslot after school? This could be something practical like jewellery-making, woodworking or demonstrating how to ice cakes, or something sporty like archery or kick-boxing (for example, Lindsey, a PA at one of our sister academies, used to run a kick-boxing class after school).

- Many PAs are involved in running some work-related training. Could you perhaps offer something like a weekly Microsoft Excel training session for other staff or a combination of staff and pupils?

- Do you have a regular timeslot in your working week when you could sit with a pupil for 20 minutes or so in the library to listen to them read aloud?

- If you have particular language skills, how about offering to help parents who have difficulties in reading and/or speaking English? You could provide a short after-school session whenever an all-school letter goes out to parents, or offer a translation service to a group of parents.

- How about volunteering to be one of the chaperones on a school daytrip?

- Next time there is a sponsored event for pupils, how about taking part in it yourself?

So, it really doesn't have to be something completely bizarre or which will require a huge effort on your part. Think of this more as doing something out of the ordinary for you.

Depending on the task, you may create better (or new) relationships with different members of the school community – pupils, parents, teachers and so on – and you will definitely find it rewarding.

So, when did you last do something that you wouldn't ordinarily do?

BRAVERY IS ... TRANSLATING
TRAINING INTO LEARNING BY
PUTTING IT INTO PRACTICE

I'm sorry to break it to you, but if you have read this far, and all you have done is read, that is not enough. It is not enough to merely read this book. You need to *act* on it, and do something with what you have learned.

You may have discovered some skills that could help you to deal with difficult situations in the workplace, but unless you put those skills into action no change will come about. You may have read about some time-saving tips and thought, 'Those will come in handy,' but until you put them into practice no time will be freed up. It's the same with your career: you won't move on in your role or new job, and a promotion won't land in your lap, without you actively doing something about it. This is what continuous professional development is all about – continuing to develop yourself from both a personal and a professional standpoint.

By far the most important aspect of any PA's, EA's, administrator's or secretary's role is to take care of the day-to-day tasks that free up their managers to get on with strategically important tasks. Many senior executives attribute as much as 40% of their productivity to their PA, so it's surprising that many managers take the view that PA training and development is not a priority for their business.

We need to maintain relevance and effectiveness in our role. This means keeping up with the latest best practice in the profession and finding ways to improve our boss's productivity. Most managers would not hesitate to sign off regular training for an accountant, yet they often fail to acknowledge the training needs of the person who holds them safely in a protected bubble on a daily basis.

How much of a struggle has it been in the past for you to get your manager to agree to letting you attend a training course or a networking event/conference/exhibition for PAs? Being able to demonstrate to your boss how much you have gained from undertaking CPD can be the key to getting them to agree to authorising more of it, particularly when they see how exceptional you can be.

In some organisations – particularly in the corporate world – staff are given CPD targets each year. In other words, they are told how many hours of CPD they should be undertaking. Even if your school, college or university doesn't have CPD targets, it's good practice for you to take stock on a regular basis to check what you have done that could be counted as active learning.

So, what have you done that could be counted as CPD? Remember, it's not just about attending courses. It's about having the willingness to learn, develop new skills and refresh existing skills. In the last year, have you done any of the following?

- Carried out online learning (e.g. searched for something, done any research via Google, watched a webinar).
- Read work-related magazines.
- Bought (and read!) work-related books.
- Trained/mentored colleagues.
- Networked with fellow PAs.

All of these can be counted as being CPD-related, *if* you have done something and learned something from it. If you have developed yourself, then it counts.

As already mentioned, I recommend that you create and use your all-important purple folder, and be sure to that you record your CPD in it (see page 117). Get into the habit of making a note in your purple folder of each new skill or technique you learn, as well as every time you find a way to do something differently. Get your boss to sign and date the note. You can use this at performance appraisals, pay reviews or job interviews to put yourself ahead of the rest. Then, most importantly, make sure you follow it up and turn your training into learning.

It is not enough just to go on a course or read a book – you need to actively use what you have learned for effective learning to take place and for change to come about. This turns the training into effective learning.

Hermann Ebbinghaus, a 19th century German scientist, proved that 'learning cannot occur without repetition' with his study into how quickly people forget and what to do to compensate for this. His 'forgetting curve' demonstrates the decline of memory retention over time when there is no attempt to retain it. Humans tend to halve their memory of newly learned knowledge in a matter of days or weeks unless they consciously review the learned material.

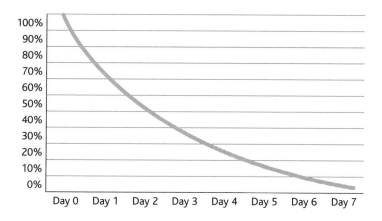

A UK survey in July 2013 asked companies to estimate what percentage of their total training budget was invested in transitioning employees from being simply trained to genuinely learning the content.[1] Some 95% of the survey's respondents said that they invested less than 10% of their total budget in 'ongoing learning after training' and 85% of those admitted to investing less than 5% – many of whom privately admitted to investing nothing at all. Unless sufficient time and effort (including budget) are invested in this activity, employees receive 'training' but they do not subsequently 'learn' the content of the training course.

This means employers are wasting millions of pounds annually on training their staff who, without adequate follow-up activity, (very) promptly forget the content of what their employers have invested in them! Further review indicated that the primary reason for the failure of line managers to invest sufficient time or any budget was because it was regarded as an 'unnecessary' and 'optional' activity.

KEEPING A RECORD

Please use the next few pages in this chapter to make notes on a monthly basis of:

- Things you have learned within your role.
- Decisions you have made.
- Commitments for further action.

You might like to include dates of training events, conferences and networking meetings, details of books or magazines you'd like to read, training sessions you'd like to offer to colleagues and so on. Sign and date the notes, and diarise to check and follow-up on your progress within a month. And remember: keep learning!

---

1   Elephants Don't Forget, *Stupid Is As Stupid Does*. Available at: http://elephantsdontforget.com/download/stupid-is-as-stupid-does/.

MONTH 1 ....

- Things learned:
- Decisions made:
- Commitments for action:

Signed: .... Date: ....

To be actioned by: ....

MONTH 2 ....

- Things learned:
- Decisions made:
- Commitments for action:

Signed: .... Date: ....

To be actioned by: ....

MONTH 3 ....

- Things learned:
- Decisions made:
- Commitments for action:

Signed: .... Date: ....

To be actioned by: ....

MONTH 4 ....

- Things learned:
- Decisions made:
- Commitments for action:

Signed: .... Date: ....

To be actioned by: ....

MONTH 5 ....

- Things learned:
- Decisions made:
- Commitments for action:

Signed: .... Date: ....

To be actioned by: ....

MONTH 6 ....

- Things learned:
- Decisions made:
- Commitments for action:

Signed: .... Date: ....

To be actioned by: ....

MONTH 7 ....

- Things learned:
- Decisions made:
- Commitments for action:

Signed: .... Date: ....
To be actioned by: ....

MONTH 8 ....

- Things learned:
- Decisions made:
- Commitments for action:

Signed: .... Date: ....
To be actioned by: ....

MONTH 9 ....

- Things learned:
- Decisions made:
- Commitments for action:

Signed: .... Date: ....
To be actioned by: ....

MONTH 10 ....

- Things learned:
- Decisions made:
- Commitments for action:

Signed: .... Date: ....

To be actioned by: ....

MONTH 11 ....

- Things learned:
- Decisions made:
- Commitments for action:

Signed: .... Date: ....

To be actioned by: ....

MONTH 12 ....

- Things learned:
- Decisions made:
- Commitments for action:

Signed: .... Date: ....

To be actioned by: ....

BRAVERY IS ... DECIDING
WHEN IT'S TIME TO PUT YOUR HANDS IN
THE AIR AND STEP AWAY FROM THE DESK

When it comes to moving on from a job, there are lots of different factors that lead us to making this tough decision.

If you don't believe wholeheartedly in your job and the team of people you are working with, my advice would be to make a change to your role, work harder at connecting better with your colleagues or leave. Do not sit in the job, hating it or not happy about what you are doing. Do something about it! Or leave.

If you have outgrown your role, if there is no opportunity for advancement or if you desperately want something more challenging that you can be passionate about, you may well be able to alleviate some of these frustrations within your existing role by taking on new responsibilities. Alternatively, you may decide that you can only get these challenges and find the passion you need somewhere else.

If your personal circumstances make it increasingly difficult for you to maintain your job, or bad health dictates that you physically or mentally cannot continue, you may not be able to change these circumstances, so leaving your job might be the only option.

If you hate the work, if it's stressful enough to make you sick, if you don't fit in, if you have the boss from hell, if you are over-qualified and bored silly or if you are asked to do something that you know is unethical or illegal, these can all be serious clues that you need to either substantially change things or that it may be time to move on.

If there is a big organisational shake-up and your role is threatened, or when the dust starts to settle you realise that you no longer fit in with the new regime, you may not be able change this. If you don't believe in what the leadership of the school or college is aiming for, it's only going to get more and more uncomfortable the longer you stay.

If you are unhappy at work, and can't see a way to solve this, it can lead to your performance suffering. You will become less productive, which then leads to feelings of dissatisfaction on both sides – you will feel unhappy, unappreciated and below par, and your leadership team will be dissatisfied because you are not doing what they want, when they want it and how they want it. Being unhappy in your work will also have an impact on your work–life balance, and you can then find yourself spending all your waking hours at home worrying about your work.

If you have found your role to be challenging, interesting and hard work, but you want to take a break to relax a bit, change your frame of mind or do something different – listen to that inner voice.

If, for whatever reason, you don't wake up most mornings with some sort of feeling of excitement or contentment about your role, change it or leave it. Nobody should stay in a job where they are unhappy (which will lead to you being miserable – trust me, I've been there a couple of times and have met countless others who have too). You will never tap your true potential if you don't love what you are doing.

If you are experiencing any of the above, it's decision time. The decision over whether you should stay and change things or leave is totally your decision, your choice. But for heaven's sake, don't just do nothing about it and sit and fester in uncertainty, unhappiness or boredom.

The only times when I would urge you to leave your role is if you are experiencing verbal abuse, sexual harassment or being bullied, and you have asked for support but nothing is being done. Nobody should be expected to put up with this in any job, so get out.

 For me, when the time came, I had to acknowledge that while I loved my last job with all my heart, my health wasn't up to it. After five surgical procedures in two years, I wasn't fit to sit at a desk for eight, nine, ten hours or more per day, and to give the job my all. I was lucky enough that a new career had been building for me in the background as I had been running training courses worldwide during holiday periods, and I had started to develop hopes of moving into training as a new career 'at some point in the future'. After the final surgery, it became apparent that the future was now – it was time to do it.

Since leaving my last role, I've been building the business so that I can continue travelling the world and working with amazing PAs on short trips which are manageable while my health improves. There are definitely days when I really miss my old job – I miss the people and I miss the pupils – and there are days when it's scary that I'm no longer in a full-time permanent job with a regular pay-cheque, but it's the most exciting rollercoaster of a ride! Who knows, if I had been in better health I may have stayed at the academy longer, but now, a year on, I know it was the right move for me. Having left my position of being a brave PA, I'm still pushing ahead, determined to be a brave PA trainer, mentor and coach.

BRAVERY IS ... LEAVING
YOUR JOB IN A PROFESSIONAL MANNER

If you are leaving your current post to take up a new role, think about what will happen when you are gone. Will any of the staff left behind know:

● Your passwords to get into various items of work?

● How to access your documents?

● Their way around your filing system?

● How to carry out the major tasks of your role?

Whether you leave under friendly terms or acrimoniously, a good PA should always leave behind adequate handover notes to allow someone to pick up the pieces after you have gone.

I've already mentioned several times the importance of creating your purple folder (see page 117) for many different reasons – now the folder can come into play when you move on to another job. Give your successor a head-start in the role by leaving them some great handover notes on how to fill your shoes.

If you are moving on from your role but you haven't yet created your purple folder (shame on you!), let's at least concentrate on making sure that you hand on some of the most important information to your successor.

Your handover notes (and steps to follow) should include:

● Your computer log-in details, including username and password.

● Details of where your computerised documents are stored (this may be the hard drive of the machine, a certain area on a network or a combination of areas, depending on the item).

● If any files are password protected, give the passwords to an appropriate-level member of staff.

- Remove any of your own personal.files from your computer/ network.

- As a courtesy, you could consider leaving your mobile/cell number so that you can be contacted if there is a query about anything.

It's a good idea to prepare this information in advance, even if you are not thinking of moving on at the moment. In this way, if you are head-hunted, suddenly struck ill, have a big win on the Lottery or are affected suddenly by redundancy – or if you *do* decide to move on and start applying for jobs elsewhere – you are already partway there to leaving adequate handover notes.

Obviously, if you are leaving the organisation due to redundancy or restructuring it can be very difficult to consider these things – which is why preparation beforehand (i.e. your purple folder) is key. In most roles in education you're likely to have the opportunity to work your entire notice period, but I've known some organisations in the corporate world who have required certain staff to leave immediately after giving notice or being made redundant, on the basis that they deem the work that the staff member carried out to be highly confidential or commercially sensitive.

WHAT ELSE SHOULD YOU DO BEFORE LEAVING?

Help your boss to put together a decent advert for your replacement, along with an appropriate job description and person specification. If you've been keeping these up-to-date regularly during your time in the role this should now be a relatively easy task. Depending on the timescales, particularly if you are leaving on a long notice period, you may even have some input into appointing the right person for the role and have a short handover period with them.

Leaving in a professional way gives you the option of returning to work for the same school, college or boss again in the future. (Over the years, I've had offers of working again with no fewer than four of my previous employers, including two who worked at completely different organisations.) Even if you don't take up a job offer from a previous employer, just knowing that they would happily hire you again can be a huge boost to your self-confidence when you come to apply for a new job. It's also something to mention at interviews elsewhere, so that your prospective new employer will realise what a valuable employee you could be to them, so valuable that your previous employers would have you back in a heartbeat.

BRAVERY IS ... FINDING A NEW PATH FOR YOURSELF AND KNOWING THAT YOUR BOSS IS BEHIND YOUR DEVELOPMENT 100%

We all undergo lots of changes in our careers: a promotion within our school, a move to another school, a complete shift to a different type of role or a different industry, or taking time out to have a child and then finding on returning to work that you would prefer to be at home with your child. Working out what your new path should be is scary and requires bravery – after all, very few people will admit to actively liking change.

Knowing that you have the backing of your boss can be a really great boost to help push you in the right direction on your new path. If you have a great working relationship with your head teacher or principal, then both of you will see that it's time for a change for you. They can then support you in the move, assist you in achieving your new goal and steer you towards appropriate assistance and advice if you are stuck. If you can both see that your career is moving and progressing, and they can support you in this, hurrah!

It can be intimidating to start filling out application forms, especially if you have been in your current role for some time and it's therefore been a while since you last applied for a role, or if you are applying for a new type of role for which you don't yet have much experience. However, if you have a boss behind you who backs your move, they can lend a hand by reading through your application or giving your some pointers on how to apply. The great working relationship you have with your head teacher (see page 159) will now come up trumps: because you are working with them in an empowering relationship (where they allow you to have a free rein over what you do and how you handle situations, allowing you to make the necessary decisions), they will also be encouraging you to take charge over where you are going with your career, and will support you wholeheartedly in it.

If you are fortunate enough to work with a great head teacher or principal in this way, you will find that they will quite often back you to the hilt in your attempts to bravely move onwards and upwards in your career.

 Here are a few examples from my own experience, where having someone else show confidence in me has pushed me beyond my imagined limits.

THE BOSS WHO SAID, 'YOU'RE NOT "JUST" AN ADMIN ASSISTANT – DON'T LET ANYONE TRY TO PUT YOU DOWN FOR WHAT YOU DO'

I started out my career in a junior administrative assistant role, and eagerly set about learning everything I could about the work of the department I was in. It wasn't a glamorous role and one of my major tasks in the first few months was very labour intensive – shuffling through several thousand pieces of paper and carefully marking up 30 A0-sized maps to plot almost 2,000 installations belonging to the company in three counties. With only one copy of each map available, accuracy was absolutely vital to ensure that everything would be correctly mapped. The large number of papers referring to each installation made the task even more arduous, particularly as they weren't stored in any particular order, making it potentially very easy to miss something. At the time, the department had just had some new computers installed – with an early spreadsheet package on them – which I set about learning how to use as I'd heard that spreadsheets were good for sorting data.

Sifting through the reports and documents, I started logging the details into a spreadsheet, ending up with a file containing the details of approximately 1,900 installations, which I then found out how to sort into grid reference order using the National Grid coordinates assigned to each installation. By pushing myself to learn a completely new application and work through the pile of data, I had developed a way to ensure that every single installation could be mapped without missing anything, and the spreadsheet details were arranged in order, matching the grid references on the maps.

My manager was overjoyed. After years of the company not having an adequate system, within just a few weeks of me being in the role there was now a dual system (of maps and matching spreadsheet grids) that could be used really easily, once I'd shown people how to use the spreadsheet package. My boss told me, 'You're not "just" an admin assistant – don't let anyone try to put you down for what you do,' words which I've remembered for more than 20 years. A few months after the spreadsheets and mapping task were finished, my manager advised me to apply for a higher role within the company and helped with my application – and I got it.

THE PROFESSOR WHO SAID, 'YOU NEED TO START LOOKING FOR A NEW JOB SOMEWHERE ELSE'

In my mid-twenties, in a role as a senior secretary at a university, I worked for a group of seven academics, the main one of whom was a female professor, whose role was enormous. It was impossible to give her just one seventh of my time and energy – ideally she needed a full-time secretary/PA all to herself. In my first year of working for her, she became dean of the School of Education and her workload increased further. A year later, she was appointed deputy vice chancellor of the university, a temporary role which lasted for two years. During the second year of her tenure, she told me that I should leave. Straight out of the blue, she just said it: 'Angela, you need to start looking for a new job somewhere else.'

I was taken aback. Had I done something terribly wrong? 'Absolutely not,' she assured me, and then she told me why. She was getting married and moving to another country at the end of the two-year deputy vice chancellor role. She could see that my role would diminish significantly at that point, as I would no longer be working for her as a professor and dean (with fingers in various pies), and the deputy vice chancellor position would be transferred to another professor elsewhere within the university, not within the group of academics I looked after. She told me, 'You have to leave around the same time I do. You won't progress further in your role here in the next few years otherwise, and I'm not going to have all the hard work I put into getting you to this level of expertise wasted. You *have* to leave and get a higher level role elsewhere!' I duly did what she suggested, and we both left the university around the same time.

Several years on, during which time I had moved to Ireland and lived there for five years, I started making plans to move back to the UK. I continued working for her on a freelance basis in my spare time, by phone and then email, and she had also moved back to the UK. I mentioned to her that I was returning to England and she offered me a job again if I was going to be moving anywhere near to her, or with her son's company if I planned to move to his end of the UK. She was totally behind me in ensuring that I moved onwards and upwards in whatever I did, and knowing this really boosted my confidence when moving back to the UK and applying for roles.

'YOU NEED TO SET UP YOUR OWN COMPANY'

In May 2009, towards the end of my first year at the academy, I was interviewed by an online PA magazine, *PA Enterprise*, on the strengths of being an avid networker (globally the most connected PA on LinkedIn), working in a school environment, singing with a band and multi-tasking in a number of different roles in my life. I remember that my boss, the principal-to-be, congratulated me and jokingly said, 'You'll be a public speaker soon,' at which I laughed. 'Oh, no, no,' I thought. I sang with a band and I could talk the hind leg off a donkey, but I wasn't a public speaker. That wasn't me at all.

The year 2010 saw me being interviewed by *NAHPA*, the National Association of Headteachers' PAs magazine, and shortlisted for PA of the Year – and I was invited to speak to my first major audience in London. My principal reminded me that he'd predicted I'd be a public speaker soon. In 2012, having been delivering courses in the UK, Ireland and Norway, he advised me, 'You need to set up your own company. Your public speaking and training work is going to build, and if you are going to make a go of it, which I think you should, you will need your own company. Get it set up now so that it will be ready.'

My company, Pica Aurum, was the result. I work to help people to achieve their goals and aims, and to reach their full potential through training, mentoring, coaching and counselling. The logo shows my favourite bird, a magpie, looking into a mirror and seeing its potential, its inner core, being reflected back in gold. The name Pica Aurum is a play on the magpie's Latin name, *Pica pica*, and *aurum*, which is Latin for gold, hence 'golden magpie'. Through the foresight of my principal at the academy, Pica Aurum is now an established brand name in the PA training arena and has been running for over three years.

BRAVERY IS ... LENDING
SOME OF YOUR BRAVERY TO OTHERS

Whatever you do with your career, whatever path you choose to take and wherever it takes you, spare a thought for your colleagues.

As the administration expert in your school or college, you are in the perfect position to assist them, so from time to time you might consider lending them the brave strengths, assets and skills from your bravery bag to help them along. Give them the benefit of your experience and expertise, share your knowledge with them, help them to become the best they can be in their roles and encourage them to strive for the best.

We are in the perfect position, working in education, to help inspire and build a new generation of PAs and administrators, so put yourself out there: offer the wealth of your expertise and experience to give somebody else a pathway into a fantastic career.

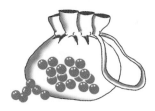

Here are some suggestions for things you could do:

- Share the idea of your bravery bag with some of your admin colleagues – be proud to tell them which bravery strengths, assets and skills you have developed in the time you've been in your role, and ask them which bravery beads they have developed in their jobs.

- I've already mentioned this a few times, but why not think about writing an article and submit it to a PA-related magazine – and then actually go ahead and do it?

- How about contacting a PA website and offering some of your expertise towards improving the content on the site?

- Hold a networking event for PAs and admins and encourage them to meet and mingle. Ask everyone to fill in a short questionnaire about their particular areas of expertise, and then (with everyone's permission) send it round to all the attendees afterwards, with contact details. This would then give everyone a chance to get in touch with someone who might be able to help them with something in the future.

- Speak with whoever runs the business studies courses at your school or college and put yourself forward to help out in some way.

- One really great thing you could do would be to become a mentor for other administrators at your school, college or university – you can learn about this via online courses, books and guides. A good mentor doesn't just tell people how to do something or provide answers – you would be empowering your colleagues to find answers for themselves. Not only will you gain a lot of satisfaction from watching someone reach their potential, but you will also learn a lot from them yourself – win-win all round!

There are several attributes and skills that you can use in order to be a good mentor to your colleagues:

- Be willing to share your skills, knowledge and expertise – teach what you know, whilst accepting whatever level of development your colleague is at personally.

- Demonstrate a confident attitude and be a positive role model – show the attitudes and actions that your colleagues need to succeed.

- Take your role as mentor seriously and invest something of yourself in your colleague's success – this shows them you have the confidence that they can develop their own strengths, beliefs and personal attributes.

- Show enthusiasm about your own role – it's catching and will transfer to your mentees!

- Make sure that you continue with your own ongoing learning and growth to demonstrate the importance of us all continuing to learn new things throughout our careers. Be committed and open to experimenting and learning practices that are new to your role.

- Offer guidance and constructive feedback, helping your mentees to identify their current strengths and weaknesses and offering them appropriate challenges in their professional development.

- Be a good role model by becoming well-respected by your colleagues – be someone for your mentee to look up to.

- Set ongoing goals for yourself, both personally and within your work, and demonstrate how to work towards success.

- Make sure that you take into account and value the thoughts, opinions, ideas and initiatives of others – be willing to share your success as part of a team.

- Motivate others by setting a good example for them to follow – be inspiring.

Bravely putting your foot forward or offering a helping hand can be the first vital part of beginning to help others, and a further step in developing yourself.

BRAVERY IS ... MOVING
ONWARDS AND UPWARDS

Finally, we reach the end of this book.

This has not been a book designed to turn you from being a PA into something else. It has not been my intention to tell you, 'Yes, yes, you are an exceptional PA now, so it's time to move on.'

The whole point of me writing this book has been to demonstrate that whilst it is quite possible that you are already absolutely brilliant in your role, there is *always* something more that you can learn.

Whether you stay in your job, progress to another role elsewhere in your school, college or university, or move on to something else entirely, my aim has been to show you that there is always room for improvement, always something different and new to be striving for. And there's certainly something that we can leave behind as a legacy to those who follow us.

 In each role that I've worked in, I tried hard to ensure that I have left something of me behind – passing on some of my knowledge and learning to other team members in the organisation or setting up a process or procedure that has outlived my time there.

My wish is that you will always work towards leaving a legacy of some sort, even if you plan to never leave. There will always come a time when you are no longer in the role – after all, we all have to retire eventually, or one day Brad Pitt/George Clooney/Johnny Depp/ whoever might finally walk into your office and say, 'Leave all this behind and come with me ...' Oh well, we can but dream!

I've loved each and every role that I've held as a PA in education, and I hope that you feel that too about your role. I've met PAs who have said that they love knowing they make a difference and that they hold a role of huge significance in ensuring that the school, college or university runs smoothly. I hope you can reach this level of satisfaction, and that you gain the recognition that you deserve for what you do. After all, credit where it's due!

From my training work around the world, it is very clear that PAs, EAs, secretaries and administrative assistants in education are a hard-working and committed group of very talented people. You are a part of the group – hold your head up and be proud.

Make sure, therefore, that you leave something of yourself behind, and make sure that the others who follow you know that they too can be brave PAs.

RESOURCES

Some fantastic resources for helping in your work are your colleagues. Also of great assistance will be other PAs in other schools, colleges and universities. In addition, there are a range of PA magazines and books, networks and websites, as well as your own tried and tested devices.

Make sure that you actually *use* these resources – there is no point in having a shelf or filing cabinet drawer full of PA books and magazines if you haven't read them or at least dipped into them from time to time.

These are just a few examples of some of the best of what's available to you. Magazines are available direct from their publishers and all of the books are available to buy via online via Amazon (among other retailers). If you attend PA conferences and events, many authors will be there with copies of their books for sale, so buy a signed copy!

I've included just a selection of resources here. As you find more, make a note of them in your purple folder and pass the details on to colleagues to help them too.

MAGAZINES

NAHPA – NATIONAL ASSOCIATION OF HEADTEACHERS' PAS

www.nahpa.org.uk

- Editor/owner Angela Garry. Subscription-based magazine, 3 issues per year. For PAs and administrators in schools in the UK. Contains no advertising.

- Having written for the magazine (under its previous owners) since 2010, and edited it since 2012, I took over ownership of the magazine from April 2015 onwards. The main aims of the magazine are to inspire and motivate, to offer relevant training information, examine up-to-date educational changes, encourage PAs to share their experiences and learn from others, point people in the right direction for useful resources for CPD and to highlight the importance of the role of PA to others in the profession, so that brave PAs throughout the UK's education system get the recognition they deserve. Articles are sourced from a range of people worldwide – PAs in education, former PAs, PA trainers, pupils, teaching staff, etc.

- Published for secondary school PAs since 2001, *NAHPA* is extending in 2015 to include administrative staff in primary and tertiary education, together with a new email discussion list for subscribers plus a private group space on LinkedIn, so that subscribers can share information/ask questions of each other.

- Website contains a subscriber-only section with information on training courses, resources, latest trends, and a guest PA blog.

- Branding: 'NAHPA is the UK's leading publication for PAs and administrators in education'.

PA LIFE

www.palife.co.uk

- Editor Colette Doyle. Free magazine, 6 to 8 issues per year. A glossy magazine for PAs in the UK. Contains advertising from a range of suppliers.

- *PA Life* produces annual comprehensive and dedicated guides which are designed to assist the busy PA with everything from finding the perfect conference venue, to car hire and worldwide travel.

- Website contains venue search and supplier search facilities, plus details of *PA Life*'s own training days and ExecSec Summit events.

- Branding: 'The UK's leading title for personal and executive assistants'.

EXECUTIVE SECRETARY

www.executivesecretary.com

- Editor/owner Lucy Brazier. Subscription-based magazine, 6 issues per year. A training journal-style magazine for PAs globally. Contains no advertising.

- Includes training articles from the world's top trainers for administrative professionals. ExecSecLive is held in March each year – a conference for all PAs from all industries and backgrounds.

- Website contains back issues of the magazine which are available to subscribers only – over 500 articles and 100+ transcripts from #adminchat training sessions.

- Branding: 'The essential training resource for senior and aspiring administrative professionals'.

EXECUTIVE PA

www.executivepa.com

- Editor Cora Lydon. Subscription-based magazine, 6 issues per year. Glossy magazine for PAs in the UK (with sister publications in Asia and Australia). Contains advertising from a range of suppliers.
- Holds an annual awards competition, in conjunction with Hays, for PA of the Year.
- Website contains back issues of the magazine which can be viewed online for free.
- Branding: 'The longest established and leading magazine brand for professional PAs'.

PA ENTERPRISE AND ADMIN ADVANTAGE

www.deskdemon.com

- Publisher/editor Paul Ormond. Free magazines available digitally by pdf file only, 11 issues per year.
- Subscribe via the website – the UK and US versions of the site and magazines contain some differences.
- The website includes an archive of all previous issues.
- Branding: 'DeskDemon's magazines for executive PAs, office managers and secretaries'.

BOOKS

Baker, Heather (2010). *Speed Writing Skills Training Course: Speedwriting for Faster Note Taking and Dictation, An Alternative to Shorthand to Help You Take Notes* (Lancashire: Universe of Learning).

Baker, Heather (2012). *Successful Minute Taking and Writing: How to Prepare, Write and Organize Agendas and Minutes of Meetings* (Lancashire: Universe of Learning).

Barron-Stubley, Susie (2012). *Create a Business-Busting Partnership With Your Assistant: The Executive's Guide* (N.p.: lulu.com).

Egan, Marsha (2008). *Inbox Detox* (Boston, MA: Acanthus Publishing) (with blog at http://inboxdetox.com).

France, Sue (2012). *The Definitive Executive Assistant and Managerial Handbook: A Professional Guide for Leadership for All Secretaries, PAs, Office Managers and Executive Assistants* (London: Kogan Page).

France, Sue (2012). *The Definitive Personal Assistant and Secretarial Handbook: A Best Practice Guide for all Secretaries, PAs, Office Managers and Executive Assistants* (London: Kogan Page).

Garry, Angela (forthcoming). *Collected Articles 2010 to 2014.*

Low-Kramen, Bonnie (2004). *Be the Ultimate Assistant: A Celebrity Assistant's Secrets to Working With Any High-Powered Employer* (New York: NK Publications).

Schwartz, Laura (2010). *Eat, Drink and Succeed: Climb Your Way to the Top Using the Networking Power of Social Events* (Chicago, IL: Black Ox Press).

Seeley, Monica (2011). *Brilliant Email: How to Win Back Time and Increase Your Productivity* (Harlow: Pearson Education) (with blog at www.mesmo.co.uk/blog).

Sokol Evans, Vickie (2013). *10 Tips in 10 Minutes Using Microsoft Office 2010 (Tips in Minutes using Windows 7 & Office 2010)* (Kindle edition). (Other volumes by the same author are available for PowerPoint, Outlook and Excel.)

PA-RELATED AND TRAINING-RELATED WEBSITES

WWW.ALISON.COM

A free training website offering diploma courses online. Create a free registration to use the site and sign up for a course. Free use of the site includes advertisements during your course sessions, or you can choose to pay for a premium subscription which will exclude the advertising. Excellent for learning some new skills – and for pointing others in the right direction for their own training.

WWW.BOOKBOON.COM

An absolutely invaluable source of free 'how to' books. Create a free registration to use the site and you can then download e-books (saved in PDF format) on an enormous number of topics, including business/office subjects. This includes comprehensive books on using the Microsoft Office suite – every package, every version – from beginner to intermediate to advanced level. A superb source of resources.

WWW.DESKDEMON.COM / WWW.DESKDEMON.CO.UK

DeskDemon is an information portal with lots of different useful sections for PAs and administrators. Launched in the UK in August 2000, DeskDemon is continually being developed in close collaboration with PAs, office managers, secretaries and administrative staff to offer a single website encompassing all aspects of office management.

WWW.PAFSA.CO.ZA

The Professional Association for Secretaries and Administrators (PAFSA), based in South Africa, led the celebrations which took place throughout the world for the International Year of the Secretary and Administrator (IYOTSA) 2014. Whilst the IYOTSA year is now over, do keep an eye on the PAFSA website for further updates relating to the PA community.

WWW.PA-ASSIST.COM

A web portal with lots of relevant suppliers and links. Sign up for their free monthly email newsletter from 'Moneypenny' – full of useful information and reminders of special dates.

NETWORKING WEBSITES

WWW.LINKEDIN.COM

The global networking site for business professionals. Everything on LinkedIn works on a three level basis: your direct connections are the first level, the people they are connected to are the second level and the people they are connected to are the third level. When you conduct a search on the site for any individual – for example, if your head teacher or college principal asks you to look up a particular candidate who has applied to your school or college for a job, or if you are searching to find an interim finance assistant to help out for a term – the reach of your search will be restricted to your three level network. If you only have a tiny network, this means that you will struggle to get any meaningful search results, whereas a much larger network gives you much more scope to find the right person.

You could spend a lot of time building up a large network on LinkedIn, or you could use a shortcut route. By connecting with a 'superconnector' (that is, someone with a very large network), their first and second level connections will become your second and third level connections. I'm the world's most connected PA and PA trainer on LinkedIn, with more than 21,000 first level and around 5 million second level connections – so, if you connect with me, that will give you an instant three level network of around 5 million people.

How to connect with me on LinkedIn:

- Join the site and create your own profile page.
- Search for 'Angela Garry' or go to: **www.linkedin.com/in/angelagarry**.
- Click the blue 'Connect' button.
- Enter my email address (angelagarry@picaaurum.com) if prompted.
- Submit to send an invitation.

Once you are on the site, I'd recommend the following discussion groups for you to join:

- PAs, EAs, VAs and Senior Administrators
- NAHPA – National Association of Headteachers' PAs
- Global Education Administration
- International School Administrators
- International School Educators
- Higher Education Administration
- Education Management Professionals
- Great Schools: Instructional Leadership Coaching & Development
- UK Education

In these groups, you have the opportunity to network with fellow PAs and educationalists, and you can post questions to seek their help and assistance. Reading some of the existing discussions in a group will give you a good feel for how the system works – so go ahead, join a group or two and start participating! There's so much you can learn from your peers.

WWW.EUMA.ORG

European Management Assistants connects over 2,000 PAs in over 25 countries across Europe. National groups hold meetings up and down their countries – one country hosts the international training day each year whilst another country hosts the International AGM and conference.

WWW.THEPACLUB.COM

London-based community of senior PAs and EAs. Founded in 2006 as a networking organisation.

MAJOR ANNUAL PA EVENTS

These are some of the major exhibitions/expos/trade fairs/PA programmes that are currently available. For the most up-to-date details on each event, check their websites for information. The events are arranged in approximate calendar order – dates are, of course, subject to variation each year.

FEBRUARY – INTERNATIONAL CONFEX AND OMPA (OFFICE MANAGER AND PA SHOW), LONDON

www.international-confex.com

www.om-pa.co.uk

International Confex connects event organisers with an exciting line-up of venues, destinations and event support services. The event includes the Office Manager and PA Show, a mix of business, networking and educational opportunities. A major event with 2,000+ PAs attending over two or three days.

FEBRUARY – BUSINESS TRAVEL SHOW, LONDON

http://www.businesstravelshow.com

A popular annual show for those of you with responsibilities for business travel for your head teacher/principal. An excellent opportunity to make connections with a wide range of business travel specialists. A major event with 2,000+ PAs attending over two or three days.

MARCH – EXECUTIVESECRETARYLIVE, LONDON

http://executivesecretarylive.com/london

Featuring top trainers for assistants, handpicked for their exceptional content and delivery. Usual attendance of around 120 PAs from across Europe.

APRIL/MAY – EXECSEC SUMMIT, USUALLY IN OXFORDSHIRE

www.forumevents.co.uk

Free event (including accommodation) for a group of selected PAs, enabling you to have one-to-one meetings with a range of suppliers/venues/services. Usual attendance of around 75 PAs and 100+ suppliers. The programme includes some training/CPD sessions.

MAY – ZOOM IN'S EXECUTIVE PA, SECRETARY AND ADMIN FORUM, DUBLIN

www.zoomin.ie

Annual conference for PAs. Attendance of around 100 PAs.

SEPTEMBER/OCTOBER – OFFICE*, LONDON

http://www.officeshow.co.uk

Annual exhibition and conference for PAs, EAs, office managers and VAs. Attendance of 3,500+ PAs over two days.

ANGELA GARRY AND PICA AURUM

 You are very welcome to use my websites for resources – training courses, details of useful books and magazines, links to other PA trainers and authors, useful websites and so on.

WWW.PICAAURUM.COM

My PA training website, includes details of my forthcoming training courses worldwide.

WWW.GOLDENMAGPIE.CO.UK

My life and career coaching and counselling website.

WWW.FACEBOOK.COM/PICAAURUM

My Facebook Pica Aurum page.

ACKNOWLEDGEMENTS

Thanks must go to my teaching and training inspirationalists: Ann Keeling who predicted when I was 12 that I would attend university; Tandy Watson who inspired me to train as a teacher; Jean Palumbo who led the first training course that I attended for PAs; and PA trainers Sue France, Rosemary Parr and Susie Barron-Stubley who planted the seed of thought that I could make a career out of training.

Workplace inspiration has come from former bosses and colleagues: Dr Stephen Bird for having faith in me and telling me I'd go far; Professor Mary John – an absolute force to be reckoned with; Dr E. Sarah Burnett – another highly inspirational woman who sadly lost her 20 year battle against cancer in 2013; Colin Hetherington and Brian Byrne, port CEOs, great bosses both; Paula Reed for encouragement and tapping into my potential; Andy Case for enthusiasm, support and his utterly fabulous drawings; Dr Matthew McFall, PhD BPhil (seriously, how many doctorates does a person need?) for laughs, Earl Grey and crab paste; and D.H., by far the most inspiring person I've ever worked for, in my most demanding role to date.

To all of the PAs, EAs, VAs and administrators I've had the pleasure of working with both throughout my PA/admin career and in my training/networking sessions. I've had the honour to meet, present to, train, mentor, coach and work with more than 2,500 of you fabulously inspiring admins all over the world. Thanks to you all for sharing your experiences, expertise, excellence, exuberance and cake!

My first forays into publishing have been thanks to: Susan Silva at *PA Enterprise* and DeskDemon; Kelly Rennie, Cath Forte and David Edwards at *NAHPA*; Lucy Brazier at *Executive Secretary*; Colette Doyle at *PA Life*; and, now, all of the team at Crown House Publishing. Thanks for putting my name (and words) in print!

Aside from my work as a PA and trainer, I'm also indebted to: Helene Hanff – your books will stay with me forever; Brené Brown, PhD – 'So glad you could make it, see you on Twitter!'; and Julia Fordham, whose music has carried me for more than 25 years.

Last, but by no means least, we get to my loved ones, my family and friends: Rachel Lynas (and Bill and Emma too), Rachael Hitchcock, Claire Maxwell, Debra Jarrett – a 'best friends list' to be envied!, my Draycott crew – Michelle and Russ Torr, Deborah Stephenson, Gail and Don Windsor (and Rosie) – I love you all lots. Gordon and Debbie: yes, I will give you cuddles, but please stop trying to sit on the laptop when mama's got work to do!

Gone, but not forgotten: dear friends Susan Clark Siefferman and Helen Heubi, plus 'woof woof' to my beloved boys eBay and Sam.

I can't mention everyone else by name – it would take too long – so, to my massive network of fabulous friends and enthusiasts, thank you.

I thank you all for the inspiration and encouragement I've gained from you, which empowered me to become a brave PA and now a brave PA trainer, coach and mentor.

ABOUT THE AUTHOR

With over 22,000 first-level contacts on business networking site LinkedIn – and a three-level network extending to more than 36 million – Angela Garry is the most connected person in the world with the job titles of 'personal assistant' and 'PA trainer'.

Angela is a fully qualified teacher with a BSc(Ed) and QTS from the University of Exeter, and has worked in administrative roles in England and Ireland since 1991, with 18 years of this in personal assistant roles. She has worked in two global banks, three universities, a sixth-form college, a water and sewerage utility, an engineering consultancy, an international seaport, a government-sponsored employment training company and an executive search company, plus her most recent role for over five years as the principal's PA at a brand new academy for 11–19 year olds in Nottingham, England.

Shortlisted for both the UK Headteachers' PA of the Year and The Times/Hays PA of the Year awards in 2011, Angela has combined her teaching and PA skills to quickly become a renowned trainer, and is now a leading expert in educational administration training.

Angela has been delivering highly successful training and networking events and seminars for PAs since 2010 around the world – including the UK and Ireland, Norway, Switzerland, Russia, United Arab Emirates, Kenya, Tanzania, South Africa, Singapore, Thailand, Hong Kong and China – offering training courses to a variety of audiences in both the corporate and educational spheres.

Since 2012, she has been a leading educational administration trainer, creating and delivering training programmes specifically designed for educational PAs, and has worked with more than 350 head teachers' PAs and administrative staff from over 250 international schools and independent schools worldwide. To date, Angela has trained, coached, mentored, presented to and worked with more than 2,500 PAs, EAs, secretaries and administrators.

In April 2012, Angela created her training company, Pica Aurum, with the aim of helping everybody find and reach their potential. Through Pica Aurum she offers training and mentoring worldwide, together with career coaching, life coaching, counselling and psychotherapy in her local area.

She is the owner, editor and writer-in-chief for NAHPA, the National Association of Headteachers' PAs magazine – the UK's leading publication for PAs and administrators working in education – and has also been a regular contributor to several other leading PA magazines, including Executive Secretary, PA Enterprise, PA Life and Executive PA.

Angela Garry is currently available for bookings worldwide.

Brave PAs is her first book.

angelagarry@picaaurum.com
www.picaaurum.com
www.goldenmagpie.co.uk

ABOUT THE ILLUSTRATOR

andycasestudios@gmail.com

Andy Case has been a professional cartoonist and illustrator since the age of 13. He has produced illustrations for books, magazines, galleries and a myriad of organisations.

This has helped his passion grow and his style mature.

andycasestudios@gmail.com
http://andycasestudios.weebly.com

TESTIMONIALS FOR TRAINING SEMINARS, MENTORING AND COACHING

COMPANIES WHO HAVE BOOKED ANGELA TO DELIVER AT THEIR EVENTS

'One of Angela's strengths that has been much appreciated by us is her clarity in presenting information. Her scope of knowledge in her area of expertise reflects in all aspects of her work. As a trainer, she is proactive, clear, lively and organised and has been much appreciated by her audience.' (Sonthaya Chutisacha, coordinator, Knowledge Source Institute, Chiang Mai, Thailand)

'Attendees at Angela's project management workshop at our conference for optimum office executives and administrative professionals gave excellent feedback on the session and would like to attend it again as a full course. We will definitely engage Angela again and highly recommend her as she added tremendous value to our conference.' (Rejoice Nhlanhla Ncube, conference organiser, Melrose Training, Johannesburg, South Africa)

'I was one of organisers of the Innova conference for PAs and administrators in Moscow, where Angela Garry was one of the six international speakers. Over 50 personal assistants and administrators from a wide range of industries in Russia attended the two-day conference, and we received great feedback from them regarding the whole event, and in particular about Angela's two seminars on pushing yourself in your role and using social networks. I recommend her highly as a motivational speaker, trainer and coach for PAs and administrators.' (Olga Shumilova, administrative director, Innova, Moscow, Russia)

UK-BASED TRAINING PROVIDERS WHO HAVE ATTENDED ANGELA'S SEMINARS

'Angela Garry is highly skilled and willing to help others, has a wonderful bubbly personality, is full of energy … She is also the most connected PA on social media by far through her action-packed networking. Angela is a role model for every PA.' (Sue France, author, national chairman for EUMA, UK)

'I had the great pleasure of interviewing Angela in my capacity as a judge of The Times/Hays PA of the Year in 2011 Awards. Angela was an exceptional shortlisted candidate and demonstrated complete commitment and passion in her role as a PA.' (Susie Barron-Stubley, managing director, Castalia Coaching and Training, UK)

'Angela is possibly the most passionate, committed and dedicated PA I have ever met. She has excellent values in life and really strives to be the very best at whatever she is doing. I have met Angela on several occasions and her knowledge in what she does is outstanding.' (Melissa Burnside, office manager, Hays, UK)

COURSE ATTENDEES AT ANGELA'S EVENTS GLOBALLY

'An excellent course, both informative and revitalising. You made each one of us feel at ease and therefore learning was more enjoyable and we felt free to communicate. I loved it.' (Lydia Kagiko, Nairobi, Kenya)

'I just wanted to write and say how much I enjoyed it. As a principal's PA myself you gave me so many handy tips and resources that I can use in my daily tasks … hopefully I will be able to attend more of your workshops in the future!' (Georgina Wilson, MPW, London, UK)

'Excellent training seminar. Thoroughly enjoyed it. Hope to see you speak again in the future.' (Rachel Perrin-Stalker, DS Smith Packaging, Warwick, UK)

'I just wanted to say a quick thank you for your great seminar … It was extremely useful and I wish I'd had that knowledge and insight when I went through the redundancy process a few years ago!' (Alison Boler, ITV, UK)

'Very inspiring and informative. Good energy, very engaging.' (Kristi Sealey, Uptown Primary School, Dubai)

'Enjoyed the course and loved meeting other PAs in similar circumstances as myself. Great fun and very inspiring – thank you Angela.' (Hazel Ajlounni, International Community School, Amman)

'Really informative. Found most of it interesting and will incorporate some ideas into my role.' (Gisella Ferri, British International School, Abu Dhabi)

'Very useful and really helped me – I will use many notices and advices.' (Mayassah Barakat, Sultan's School of Muscat)

'It is great to hear points of view from a successful professional PA like Angela. It makes me look forward to improve myself.' (Debra Youplub, Bangkok Patana School, Thailand)

'Made me feel that to be a PA is valuable!' (Supantra Sinsomboon, NIST, Thailand)

'I am inspired to share my knowledge with my colleagues at school.' (Enkhee Dambaryenchin, International School of Ulaanbaatar, Mongolia)

'Very beneficial to me and my future work.' (Yana Kan, Dulwich College, Suzhou, China)

'Happy to know many participants from other countries who share my job difficulties and expectations. Clearly presented. Angela is a very humorous person.' (Winnie Yang, ISF Academy, Hong Kong)

'Angela delivered the course with great knowledge and humour. A good two days with her and useful to relate with other PAs and learn what other schools do.' (Juana Elizalde, Chinese International School, Hong Kong)

'Angela is a very lovely, friendly lady. Her training methods are amazing.' (Eleven Gu, Dulwich College, Suzhou, China)

'Really good, useful. Angela is very humorous and I found myself nodding and agreeing with so many of her stories. A good use of my time and much learned.' (Janette Roberts, St Joseph's Institution International, Singapore)

'I will definitely use the knowledge learned to better practice in my role as a PA. At the end of the training I am not just a PA but I am a Particularly Ambitious PA!' (Rozlina Jamil, Chatsworth International School, Singapore)

'I enjoyed sitting under a renowned PA and will take some of her teaching to implement at my workplace.' (Claudia Kang, Dalat International School, Penang, Malaysia)

'Angela has inspired me on the values of a PA role and her knowledge and experience is immense.' (Aliece Varughese, Tanglin Trust School, Singapore)

TOPIC INDEX

You may prefer to read from this from start to finish – or to dip in and out of it at your leisure. Alternatively, you may like to pick out chapters on a particular topic – in which case this topic index should help.

Topic	Bravery is ...	Subheading	Page	✓
Leaving your role	Leaving ...	your job in a professional manner	215	
Making the tea	Understanding ...	you're not 'too good' to make tea and coffee	47	
Managing your manager	Managing ...	your working relationship with your boss	159	
Moving on	Finding ...	a new path for yourself and knowing that your boss is behind your development 100%	219	
Moving on	Moving ...	onwards and upwards	227	
Networking	Encouraging ...	PAs to meet and network	51	
New challenges	Bracing ...	yourself for new challenges and daring to do something differently	67	
Out of the ordinary	Taking ...	on tasks that wouldn't be expected in a corporate PA job	25	
Paper vs. technology	Papering ...	over the cracks when the technology breaks down	135	
Project work	Backing ...	into the number (to find the right path to follow)	147	
Saying no	Knowing ...	when to say 'no' to the boss	125	
Starting out	Enlightening ...	– some light-hearted advice for a new PA	9	
Starting out	Getting ...	off to a great first start	15	
Starting out	Stepping ...	into your first role in an educational environment	5	
Time management	Controlling ...	the enormous number of demands on your time	107	
Time saving	Discovering ...	different ways to save time on tasks	55	